D1189561

The Trinity and Our Moral Life

according to St. Paul

The Trinity
and Our Moral Life

according to St. Paul

by CESLAUS SPICQ, O.P.

Translated by Sister Marie Aquinas, O.P.

ST. BEDE COLLEGE
—
PERU, ILL.
—
LIBRARY

The Newman Press · Westminster, Md.
1963

BX 2350.2 . S413

Nihil obstat: Rev. Edmund Siedlecki
                    Censor librorum

Imprimatur: Rt. Rev. Msgr. George J. Casey
                    Vicar General of the Archdiocese of Chicago

                    June 6, 1963

The Nihil Obstat and Imprimatur are official declarations that a book
or pamphlet is free of doctrinal or moral error. No implication is con-
tained therein that those who have granted the Nihil Obstat and Imprimatur agree with the contents, opinions or statements expressed.

Copyright © 1963 by The Missionary Society of Saint Paul the Apostle
       in the State of New York

Library of Congress Catalog Card Number: 63–12232
Printed in the United States of America

Foreword

PHILIPPI IN MACEDONIA WAS THE FIRST EUROPEAN CITY to hear the message of the Gospel. St. Paul himself had preached it there in the year A.D. 50 (Acts 16:12). At that time the core of the population was formed by soldiers that Mark Antony had disbanded a century earlier and by a contingent of settlers sent from Italy by Octavian. Octavian had granted this military "colony" the privilege of ruling itself according to "Italian law"; it had thus gradually become an autonomous administrative center modeled after a Roman city. The civil and religious institutions of Philippi, in particular the cult of the emperor, were identical to those in Rome. Magistrates had the same titles and exercised the same functions as those the capital of the empire, i.e., quaestors, lictors, duumvirs, etc. Latin was the official language as well as the language of administrative acts. The city enjoyed "liberty" and so was exempt from provincial taxes and from personal contributions. The right of property was recognized there in all its fullness, including the acquisition, the holding, and the transfer of possessions. Even the architecture and the layout of the city contributed toward making this colony a little Rome, and its inhabitants were more than a little proud to recall their origin and their rights: "We are Roman!" (Acts 16:21). Indeed, at this period, to be a Roman citizen meant to have a citizenship good throughout the Empire.

Taking these circumstances and this mentality into

account, St. Paul wrote to the Christian community at Philippi: "As for us, our commonwealth is in heaven" (Phil. 3:20). We are the beneficiaries of nobility, protection, and order, of all the advantages that such a glorious city assures its members (Gal. 4:26). Here on earth we are a group of emigrants, a colony far from our true fatherland (Heb. 11:14, 13:14). United by a common origin, we enjoy the same rights and privileges. In the days of St. Paul, those excluded from citizenship were ruled by the "law of nations," accorded both to citizens and to foreigners under the protection of Roman law; the "civil law," however, concerned the citizens alone and applied only to them. With this in mind St. Paul reminds us that *noblesse oblige*; we who are citizens of heaven must do honor to the nationality that was conferred on us by baptism and consequently lead a celestial life.

The spirit of Christian ethics is defined by this institutional and religious frame of reference: "Only let your lives be worthy of the Gospel of Christ" (Phil. 1:27), the Gospel being nothing other than an exposition of the constitution and laws of the city of heaven, promulgated by its unique sovereign, Jesus, the Savior. "To live as a citizen" means to fulfill the obligations fixed by the legislation and customs of a city, to have its mentality, and to submit to its decrees; it means to conduct oneself in such a way that everyone may recognize from a man's actions to what city he belongs (2 Mach. 6:1; Acts 23:1.) This is exactly the opposite of "living as one pleases."

Since Christians profess to belong body and soul to their Lord—this is the whole of the act of faith—St. Paul asks each one of us to live in a manner worthy of the Lord (Col. 1:10; 2 Tim. 2:12), of God (1 Thess. 2:12), of our vocation (Eph. 4:1), and of the saints, who, purified from sin and consecrated to God, form the Christian Church (Rom. 16:2; Eph. 2:19). This means, above all, to live in union with Christ and in fraternal charity, these being the specific marks of a life regulated entirely according to the norms of the Gospel. But, in a more general way, our moral life is determined by our nationality—and what a singular one it is! We are of heaven, the highest and the holiest of states. For Christians, then, the moral life consists in "living as citizens" of the "city of the living God" (Heb. 12:22). And how are we to do this? In the following pages we shall examine St. Paul's answer to this question.

Acknowledgments

The translator and The Newman Press wish to thank the following publishers for permission to make use of Scriptural quotations in the present volume:

The Bruce Publishing Company for excerpts from *The New Testament* by James A. Kleist, S.J., and Joseph L. Lilly, C.M.

The Confraternity of Christian Doctrine for selections from the Confraternity Edition of *The Holy Bible* and *The New Testament*.

Contents

Contents   xvii

The Trinity and Our Moral Life

according to St. Paul

CHAPTER 1

The Necessity of a Revealed Morality

WHAT THE PROMULGATORS OF THE GOSPEL ANNOUNCED in the first century after Christ was the Good News of Salvation—deliverance from sin and evil through the love of God as shown by the gift of His Son. It was an answer given to the anxious waiting of all men "who sit in darkness and in the shadow of death, to guide their feet into the path of peace" (Luke 1:79).

This was a dark and tragic period, if we are to believe the documents that have come down to us from Lucretius, Petronius, Juvenal, Martial, Suetonius, Apuleius, etc. Everywhere moral standards were in decline. The Greco-Roman world of the first century was characterized by ambition, cruelty, and cynicism in public office and by general decadence in private life. There was unchecked pursuit of selfish interests on the part of the rich, widespread contempt of the weak, frantic pleasure-seeking, and unlimited licentiousness. Marriage was held in derision; rape and adultery were common; homosexuality and robbery were rampant; divorces and murders, cases of infanticide and abortion were multiplied; all passions were indulged. There was a veritable epidemic of suicides. But, one might object, these facts belong to all periods, and private documents—epitaphs, papyri, graffiti—assure us that virtue continued to flourish in many pagan homes[1] and that magnanimous souls were not lacking.

What is true is that thoughtful men reflected about the meaning of life, their right to happiness, and their manner of living. The concept of conscience, at the beginning of the Christian era, grew more refined. It was no longer some horrible, vindictive divinity, but rather an inner demand for moral goodness and integrity, an attempt to regulate the actions of men in conformity with an ideal they more or less clearly perceived. But even these souls were broken on the wheel of suffering, which is an inescapable part of existence itself. Its forms were multiple: men were betrayed or oppressed by a hostile society; mothers mourned their children; wives lost their husbands; there was anguish over the lack of daily bread, over villages and fields devastated by civil or foreign wars or by the scourges of nature; there were the burdens of old age that gradually destroys all ties with this life. Everywhere disorder. And man's powerlessness to free himself from these evils was only too apparent. . . .*

* Herodotus puts these words into the mouth of a Persian, who bursts into tears while pronouncing them: "There is no greater torture for man than to see clearly without being able to do anything." The poet Simonides laments: "The strength of man is slight; none of his projects succeeds; his short life is only a succession of pains; and death, inevitable death, hangs over him." We pass on like leaves, and our thoughts are futile. "Innumerable are the misfortunes of man," writes Hesiod. "The earth is filled with evils. . . . Sicknesses besiege us day and night; they assail us silently, these bearers of calamity. No one escapes from his destiny." "All of us, as long as we live, are only phantoms, vain shadows" (Sophocles). "Race of mortals, your life is equivalent to nothingness! To speak truly, who has known a happiness other than the illusion which he has spun for himself? It dissipates itself and then disappears" (Idem.). "We enjoy our youth but a short time, just as the sun shines but briefly on the earth. When these years have

"All these themes: fatality, death, the difficulty of living, abandonment by the gods, in a word, the solitude of man staggering alone in the dark, formed the basis of Greek pessimism."[2] Where was help to be found? How were these evils to be cured? To be sure, men with ready answers were not lacking. "Enjoy yourself," said some; "toil," cried others; "live for yourself"; or the opposite, "give of yourself, and if need be, sacrifice yourself for others."

But how was a man to overcome this feeling of desolation, this disgust with life? More importantly, how could he adopt a moral attitude which was completely arbitrary, independent as it was of all reason or hope? Men had to know why they must react against weariness. They wanted to be happy, but what was the use of making an effort if experience assured them of failure? "All men are so tired and indifferent that no one deigns to lift his eyes toward the luminous regions of heaven" (Lucretius). It was commonly admitted, in fact, that an inexorable fatality, without intelligence or love, ruled all. This was

---

ended, it is better to die immediately than to go on living, for a thousand evils besiege our soul. . . . There is not a man to whom Zeus does not send a thousand misfortunes" (Mimnermus of Colophon). "Who can laugh on the way to execution? We play, but the fear of slavery strangles us; we laugh, but choked always by the fear of death." Therefore, since sorrow strikes all mortals, since disorder is the law of this world and it is impossible for a man ever to regain his courage, "it is better for him not to be born; and if he is born, to return as soon as possible into the kingdom of night" (Aristotle).

destiny (*heimarmenê*), necessity (*anankê*), inflexible fate
(*moira*), before which even the gods ceased to struggle.
They themselves could not save a mortal when the spectre
of destiny overtook him; they too mourned the loss of
creatures dear to them. Each man received his lot. He
could not change it. If he did not accept it willingly, still
he had to undergo it. All this made of the world an un-
lighted prison where men felt themselves to be held in
chains. Instead of a royal liberty, the prerogative of
spiritual beings, man developed the slave mentality of one
subject to the caprices of a tyrant.

   Obviously, men reacted differently according to tem-
perament and circumstances. Epicurus, who was ordi-
narily better inspired, dared to write: "The root of all
good is the pleasure of the belly." And again, "I spit on
morality and on the empty flattery conferred on it when
it produces no pleasure." Some tried to cultivate indifference, such as the deceased who had had inscribed on
his tomb: "I was not; I became; I have been; I am no
longer; that is all." "O my soul, do not aspire to immortality, but exhaust the realm of the possible" (Pin-
dar). Among the noblest minds, some strove for *ataraxia*,
the state of a soul exempt from trouble, desire, or passion
and no longer thinking or feeling. "Sleep, my baby, and
may the sea sleep, and may our immense misfortune also
sleep" (Simonides). Others took refuge in skepticism:
"We are the playthings of empty fables" (Euripides).

"Everything is slowly dying and is moving toward the grave, worn out by the length of life's path" (Lucretius). But the majority of men succumbed to anguish and despair. Convinced that they were being handed over defenseless to evil forces, they sought to flee from the dark prison and to escape to another world. They looked for a reason to go on living and aspired to deliverance, to "salvation."

At this juncture we see the role of the innumerable religions which abounded everywhere in the Empire—the imperial religion of the "savior-gods," demotic and traditional cults, Oriental divinities such as the Egyptian, Syrian, Phrygian, the Dionysiac, and others; also that of the masters of thought—philosophers, rhetors, grammarians, sophists, and even astrologers and magicians, such as Elymas, who was chaplain to Sergius Paulus, proconsul of Cyprus (Acts 13:6–8), or the charlatan-doctor Asclepiades, or, finally, alchemists like Zosimus. Piety and speculation, mysticism and rationalism joined forces or succeeded one another in an attempt to explain the order in the world, to give reasons for living, and to respond to men's desire of security and happiness.

These "intellectuals" fell into many categories. Some were authentic scholars, instructed in the natural and physical sciences, who sought to understand the laws of nature; others were orators, pure "littérateurs," who made pompous and empty declamations; almost all of them claimed to be possessors of a hidden wisdom and to enjoy revelations that permitted them to discover the secrets of the future. Stoic philosophers, setting themselves up as directors of conscience, sought to give a moral education—how to fortify one's soul, how to bear sorrow, how to despise death. On the other hand, magicians, so-called "wise men," were in turn wonder-workers, sorcerers, and enchanters who claimed to control the help of the celestial powers against the spirits of darkness. In Palestine the Pharisees, who were specialists in the Law and its complexities, despised the common people, the unlearned, who could not be pious because they were incapable of knowing and observing each iota of the Torah; so too the Greek "connoisseurs" or "gnostics," strong in their erudition and their specialization in mystical sciences, prided themselves on being the only holders of wisdom, of the unique saving knowledge that remained inacessible to the uninitiated (cf. 1 Cor. 2:1).

How could a man of good will discover the truth among so many masters, masters whom Jude was later to describe as deluded and wandering stars "whose mouths utter arrogant words and who flatter people to serve their own ends" (Jude 16)? Socrates had once addressed this reproach to Hippias: "That you, the wise men, are subject to change, that is what is terrible for us, for thus we have recourse to you in vain; we will not be freed from our incertitudes" (Plato, *Hipp. min.*, 376 c). St. Augustine listed three hundred fifty opinions of the philosophers on the "Sovereign Good"! But at the end of so many speculations and vain searchings, skepticism only increased. Some philosophers taught that the gods lived in perfect happiness but were indifferent to human affairs, unconcerned with mortals who were being crushed by the millstone of destiny and pulverized by the teeth of death (Lucretius). There was no Providence. Others taught that the earth was completely cut off from the heavens and that it was impossible to enter into relations with the transcendental divinity. Finally, there were "atheists," sacrilegious philosophers who denied even the existence of the gods.

> Either God wants to suppress evil but cannot do so, or he both wants to and is able to. If he wants to, but cannot, then he has no power, which is irreconcilable with God. If he neither wants to nor is able to, he has neither power nor love, and he is therefore not God. If he wants to and is able to, and this is the only solution which is fitting, then where does evil come from and why does he not suppress it? (Epicurus).

God was dead!

There is more than an atrocious blasphemy in these far too superficial reflections. There is an avowal of the fundamental failure of thinking humanity. These pagan philosophers and orators—like the professors, publicists and journalists of our day to whom is attributed the pompous title of "intellectuals"[3]—misled their disciples. Intelligence is made to discover truth, and the mouth to proclaim it; but these intellectuals deceived themselves and then published their lies. Blind and leaders of the blind, bad shepherds, they carry the terrible responsibility of having turned all humanity away from God, when they were qualified to know Him and their gifts had designated them to instruct others. From the opening words of the Epistle to the Romans, St. Paul stigmatizes the catastrophic influence of these teachers of error with extreme severity, especially since failure to recognize the true God, as the Book of Wisdom (14:12–31) had already taught, is at the origin of all moral perversions:

> The wrath of God is being revealed from heaven against all ungodliness and wickedness of those men who in wickedness stifle the truth of God. Here is the reason: what may be known about God is manifest to them, because God has manifested it to them. Since the creation of the world his invisible attributes are clearly seen—especially through his everlasting power and divinity, which are understood through the things that are made. And so they are without excuse, because although they knew God, they did not glorify him as God or give thanks, but their reasonings became absurd, and their senseless minds were darkened. While professing to be wise, they became fools, and they exchanged the glory of the incorruptible God for an image made like to corrupt-

ible man and to birds and four-footed beasts and creeping things. Therefore God has given them up, in the lustful desires of their heart, to uncleanness, so that they dishonor their own bodies—they who exchanged the truth of God for a lie and worshipped and served the creature rather than the Creator who is blessed forever, amen.

For this cause God has given them up to shameful lusts; for their women have exchanged natural intercourse for what is against nature, and in the same way men too, having given up natural intercourse with women, have burned in their lusts for one another, men with men practicing that well-known shamelessness and receiving in their own persons the fitting punishment of their perversity. And as they resolved against having a good knowledge of God, God has given them up to a seared conscience so that they do what is morally disgraceful. They are steeped in dishonesty, wickedness, greed, ill-will; they are overflowing with envy, murderous intent, strife, deceit, rancor; they secretly spread false reports; they openly calumniate, they hate God, they are insulting. They are proud, vain, boastful, ingenious in evil, disobedient to parents. They lack conscience, constancy, affection, piety. Although they are aware of the decree of God that those who do such things are worthy of death, they not only do them, but applaud others who do them. (Rom. 1:18–32).[4]

It is impossible to read this indictment without being

struck by its similarity to the diatribes of profane authors. St. Paul does not blacken his contemporaries any more than the cultured pagan writers did. But what is especially noteworthy is his condemnation of thinkers—they are inexcusable—and of the sins of intellectualism, which have had such serious and discreditable sequels and have provoked the divine anger. An authentic knowledge of God was accessible to men. The light of reason can discover the Creator in His universe and the Author in His work (Acts 14:15–17, 17:24–27). But these "philosophers" either emptied the world of God and, as a consequence, found themselves incapable of giving it a meaning; or they went off into abject caricatures of the One God, such as polytheism and idolatry (Wis. 14:12–14). Since intelligence is, in man, the highest faculty, sins of the mind are the gravest of all. In relation to faith, the highest object of knowledge is God. Therefore, since the "thinkers" "did not know God," they committed the worst of perversions. It is in the resulting darkness that all moral disorders have been loosed.

According to St. Paul the sin of intellectualism is not only the personal sin of the masters who ignored the truth when they had the mission to unveil it, but it is also a form of scandal, the greatest crime after apostasy! Those who had the mission to teach and the obligation of enlightening the less gifted, dragged them instead into error.[5] Naturally, many of those masters were in good faith and their mistakes would be excusable had they not been propagated. But publicity, given to wild dreams, sanctions interpretation and gives rise to monstrous actions. Masters who are not perfect necessarily form bad disciples, and a slight initial deviation soon produces serious aberrations.

The Old Testament and our Lord Himself denounced the lies of false prophets. St. Paul, noting the ravages they cause, vigorously put the Christians on guard against their influence and their doctrine.[6] In the Pastorals he paints a portrait of them that remains true for all centuries, and especially for our own. False prophets are characterized by independence, indocility, and obstinacy—no one can convince an intellectual who trusts in his own genius; they turn their ears from the truth, resisting it and opposing it; in the end, they are deprived of it. They are men who have gone astray.[7] Swollen with vanity and ambition (1 Tim. 6:4), they claim to have arrived at a superior knowledge; they set themselves up as teachers, although they know nothing.[8] For, even though they are always engaged in study—they are specialists in the things of the mind—they are always incapable of reaching truth (2 Tim. 3:7), and they "understand neither what they say nor the points on which they put so much stress" (1 Tim. 1:7); they are impostors (2 Tim. 3:13).

Scholars working alone in their study can be pardoned for taking a wrong turn; but these "intellectuals" are in-

cessant mouthers of empty phrases, inveterate publicists.
They have, as it were, an itch to propagandize and they
travel the world over searching for new listeners; lovers
of controversy and polemics, they stir up doubts[9] that
infect the healthy ideas of their readers or listeners like
gangrene.[10] How could St. Paul fail to excoriate such de-
ception? Pseudo-intellectuals are "vain babblers" (Tit.
1:10), having false and unhealthy minds; lacking in common sense, they are true madmen, incapable of cultivat-
ing a taste for sound and balanced doctrine.[11]

Nor are these only diatribes of an apostle; the faithful themselves were convinced of their truth. The *Acts of
the Roman Martyrs* recount that, under the Emperor
Commodus, the Christian Apollonius, when dragged before the tribunal of the proconsul, found himself obliged
to listen to the arguments of a popular philosopher. He
answered, "In the mouth of a hypocrite, truth itself is
transformed into verbiage and blasphemy." And the martyrs gave their lives while proclaiming, "We have en-
countered truth," truth which is not of this world. Such
was the Bishop Philias who declared before his judge: "I
die for God and for truth."

Against these speculators, writers, and lecturers who
deceived souls, God founded a Church destined to be
"the pillar and bulwark of truth" (1 Tim. 3:15). In
His Church salvation was not to come from intellectuals,
but from preachers; not from research and mental gym-

nastics, but from a fact, from the person of Jesus Christ. It was no longer to be a question of knowing, but of believing. The apostles were witnesses of Christ and by virtue of this, lights of the world. Their message was not one devised by human wisdom, more or less persuasive in its appeal (1 Cor. 2:1-5), but the transmission of the very word and power of God: "We are, therefore, Christ's ambassadors; we know that God makes appeal through us" (2 Cor. 5:20). "We speak in the presence of God in Christ" (2 Cor. 12:19). In God's Church salvation would still depend on a doctrine and on knowledge, but these would no longer be of human origin; since the wisdom of men is imperfect, God in person would teach each one (1 Thess. 4:9). "No longer will fellow citizens have to teach one another, or brother his brother, saying 'Know the Lord,' because all, from the least to the greatest, shall know me" (Heb. 8:11). God was speaking through the mouth of His representatives; therefore, for those who heard the message the only attitude possible was that of acceptance, "the submission of faith" (Rom. 1:5, 16:26). It was no longer a question of speculating or even of understanding more or less profoundly, according to the varying capacities of each intelligence, but of adhering and of submitting. "We demolish human calculations, yes, every fortified height that rears itself against the knowledge of God. We bring every thought into captivity under obedience to Christ" (2 Cor. 10:5).

When St. Paul preached Christ, the crucified and risen Savior, he addressed himself to all pagans, "those who are on the road to destruction," those captivated by "the seductiveness of evil" (2 Thess. 2:10), and those swept along by all the lies of masters whose thoughts "the god of this world [Satan] has blinded" (2 Cor. 4:4). How could men who had strayed so far have their vision restored? How could they discover salvation and recognize the authentic word of the true God in the preaching of the Apostle? It was all a matter of the heart's being open to grace, coupled with profound good will and especially with complete straightforwardness. It was a question of receiving *the love of truth*," which God offered to each one in order *to be able to be saved*" (2 Thess. 2:10). According to St. Paul and the whole of the New Testament, salvation or perdition is accomplished according as the soul accepts or refuses the light. The proclamation of the Gospel was addressed to all men, but only those adhered to it who, to begin with, esteemed truth and sought it above all else. From the moment that souls were faithful to this first grace infused by God, they were already oriented toward salvation, even before hearing the preaching of the Gospel. They had a cult of the true and the will to follow it. In other words, the eternal destiny of these men was decided less by an objective knowledge of the true religion than by a secret choice already determined by their moral attitude. God incited them to love, to seek, to appreciate truth, and from that time onward they were ready to adhere to the truth of the Gospel when it was revealed. To believe in God is "to believe in the truth" of His word (2 Thess. 2:13). Those who closed their souls to the inclination of grace became a prey to the "deceits" of Satan (2 Thess. 2:9). From this we see that salvation is accomplished fundamentally in terms of a first love, and not in terms of knowledge or of philosophical speculation. The love of truth is at the basis of an adherence of faith. When St. Paul affirms that faith and fidelity save, he is speaking of that total gift of self which engages the heart as much as the mind. One arrives at this identification of truth only if one has first of all loved it for its own sake, as an absolute, which admits of no compromise. The verb "to love" employed here is that related to *agape*, which signifies fundamentally to respect, to honor, to value highly, and to welcome. To say consequently that one loves the truth in charity is to say that one prefers it to everything else, even to oneself, and that one is ready to sacrifice all in order to gain it. Salvation and the Christian life take their beginning in the *caritas veritatis!*

This is so true that every manifestation of the Christian life will be conditioned by this initial charity, i.e., this religious love, which has the force of a consecration and which forbids all contamination with error and falsehood.

> We shall no longer be children tossed to and fro and
> carried about by every wind of doctrine, which wicked
> men devise with the ingenuity and cleverness that error
> suggests. Rather by professing the truth let us grow up
> in every respect in love and bring about union with
> Christ who is the head. . . . In this way the body grows
> and builds itself through love (Eph. 4:15–16).

To profess the truth is to affirm it publicly and to conform to it in practice and at the same time to prove it, as
it were, by putting one's conduct in harmony with one's
convictions. This exact fidelity to the divine thought and
will is what the Old Testament calls "walking in truth."
But the qualification "in charity" is specifically Christian.
It means far more than that the Christian is both true
and charitable (cf. Eph. 6:23) and lives as an authentic
believer, uniting orthodox faith and love. St. Paul teaches
that the new life is inspired and impregnated by charity,
a response of love to the love with which God and Christ
first loved us (cf. Eph. 5:2). What is more important,
this initial divine charity is from now on infused into the
souls of the faithful, directing them and establishing them
in right relation to their God. "Christ dwells through faith
in your hearts, so that you are rooted and grounded in
charity" (Eph. 3:17). To the same degree that "children
are tossed to and fro and carried about by every wind of
doctrine which wicked men devise with the ingenuity and
cleverness that error suggests," so Christians, who have

arrived at spiritual maturity, are solid and strong. (Eph. 4:14). Indeed, profession of "truth in charity" implies this stability and this strength. As Christians, we attach ourselves to truth and remain loyal to it by means of the bond of charity, which is the love of God and of Christ, and which impels and constrains us (2 Cor. 5:14). "To profess the truth in charity" is St. Paul's most successful formula of the moral life, which is a religious moral life. Exalting rectitude, it echoes the spirituality of Israel: "He conducts the just by right ways," and brings this spirituality to completion in divine charity, which is infused into our hearts by the Holy Spirit who is given to us through Christ. In addition it underlines the internal dynamism of a life made to grow. *To profess the truth in charity* is at one and the same time to respond by a loving fidelity to the love of God for us—the *veritas vitae*—and to submit to the law of growth that will make of imperfect little children adults vitally incorporated into Christ.

The moral life of Christians is essentially union with the person of Christ. This life supposes a conversion, which is first of all faith in the message and in the work of the redemption of the Savior and then deliverance from error. Salvation is a liberation both from sin and from the seductions of falsehood and the enticements of false masters. "God," according to St. Cyprian, "loves confessors, not propagandists." In the measure in which the faithful progress in their Christian life, they become

more aware of the treasure that they have acquired in
"the exact knowledge of truth."[12] They know that the
object of their faith is the only unchanging and complete
truth, revealed by God Himself. They understand that
this truth is religious and moral and that it requires their
unconditional adherence. It is not only a matter of con-
fessing a *credo*, but of giving one's heart and of conse-
crating one's life. "To profess the truth in charity" is
reserved to disciples of Christ, who, as the light of the
world, has revealed the love of the Father. We are
faithful to this morality when we love divine truth religiously and live by it. Our goal is to draw ever nearer to
it, to grasp it better, and to assimilate it; for God has
chosen us "that we should exist holy and without blemish
in his sight in love" (Eph. 1:4).

> It is written, "I will destroy the wisdom of the wise, and
> the cleverness of the clever I will thwart." Where is
> the "wise" man? Where is the scholar? Where is the phi-
> losopher of this world? Has not God turned into non-
> sense the "wisdom" of this world? Since the world with
> all its "wisdom" did not attain to the knowledge of God
> from his wisdom (reflected in creation), it pleased God
> by the absurdity [of the cross] we preach to save those
> who believe (1 Cor. 1:19–21).

CHAPTER 2

From the Father

REVEALED MORALITY DIFFERS ESSENTIALLY FROM ALL human ethical systems. Human ethics defines good and evil, determines conduct, and weighs values in terms of man's perfection and happiness; it is essentially "anthropocentric"; the "good life" refers to existence in an earthly city. Revealed ethics, on the other hand, is "theocentric"; it judges everything in terms of God. Man has meaning only with regard to his Creator, who is both his last end (1 Cor. 8:6) and his unique Master and Lord, who has the right to impose His will upon him and to direct his life. For this reason, revealed ethics is first of all a matter of obedience and fidelity.

Seen in this light, the history of humanity appears as a monstrous rebellion of creatures against their God. "All have sinned" (Rom. 3:23, 5:12). The Chosen People as well as pagans are "slaves of sin" (Rom. 6:16–22); and sin reigns over them as the most despotic and cruel of tyrants: "For we ourselves were once without understanding, without obedience, deceived, slaves to various lusts and pleasures. We lived in malice and envy; we were hateful and hating one another" (Tit. 3:3; cf. Gal. 5:19–21). Corruption is universal; coming from Adam whose fault has been transmitted to his descendants, it has infected human nature: "Through one man sin entered into the world. . . . By the offense of one, the many died. . . . By the disobedience of one man the many were constituted sinners" (Rom. 5:12–19).

The Law of Moses had been given to guide the Israelites toward God and to make their steps secure; but because it multiplied precepts without giving the strength necessary to accomplish them, the condition of its subjects became so much the harder. It did indeed make the determination of good and evil explicit; but this clearer knowledge of obligation so difficult to accomplish resulted in an increase of infractions which, from that time on, became overt rebellion against God. "The wisdom of the flesh is hostile to God, for it is not subject to the law of God nor can it be. And they who are carnal cannot please God" (Rom. 8:7–9).

Concupiscence, the source of all vices, grows greedier when faced with interdictions and prohibitions. That which yesterday had no attraction becomes, now that it is inaccessible, the object of an increasingly impatient desire:

> While we were ruled by our lower nature, sinful passions, aroused by the Law, were at work in our members so that they brought forth fruit for death. . . . Yet I had not known sin save through the Law. For I had not known lust unless the Law had said, "You shall not lust." But sin, having seized a base of operations in the commandment, produced in me by its means all manner of lust, for without law sin lies dormant. Once I too was without law, but when the commandment came, sin was stirred to life, and I died. Thus the commandment

that was to lead to life, was discovered in my case to lead to death (Rom. 7:5–10). The Law intervened that the offense might become greater (Rom. 5:20).

These are not historical considerations or abstract speculations. St. Paul has in mind three categories of souls: the "pure," i.e., those who are unconscious of the real nature of their actions, the pseudo-just who believe themselves blameless; secondly, deliberate or inveterate sinners who call good, evil, and evil, good, and who lack the sense of submission that all creatures must have before the God who created them; and finally, those without hope, who groan under the weight of faults from which no one can free them. St. Paul convinces the first of their wickedness, the second of the gravity of their blindness, the last of the possibility of their cure. Because he, too, experienced the conflict between conscience and lust, St. Paul understands sin. In the following passage he personifies it as a principle alien to his nature, a foe ever active within and finally victorious:

I am carnal, sold into slavery to sin. Why, I do not understand what I do, for what I wish, I do not; what I hate, I do. But if I do what I do not wish, I admit that the Law is good. But then it is no longer I who do it, but the sin that dwells in me. Well do I know that in me, that is, in my lower nature, no good dwells, because to wish is within my power, but I do not find the strength to accomplish what is good. Yes, I do not do the

good that I wish, but the evil that I do not wish, that I
do. Now if I do what I do not wish, it is no longer I who
do it, but the sin that dwells within me. Therefore, when
I wish to do good, I discover this to be the rule, that evil
is ready at hand. My inner self agrees joyfully with the
Law of God, but I see another law in my bodily members warring against the Law which my mind approves
and making me prisoner to the law in my members which
allures me to sin. Unhappy man that I am! Who will
rescue me from this body doomed to death? (Rom. 7:
14–24).

Infelix homo! This is the cry of the sinner who, although he has momentary pleasures, cannot find apart
from God the happiness to which he aspires with all his
might (Rom. 8:18–25). More strictly than the armed
cherubim guard the gates of paradise, his own faults for-
bid him access to this beautiful hidden kingdom until
the day when he hears resounding in his ears the liberat-
ing words of the apostle of Christ: "Your sins are forgiven
you"! To believe these words is to believe that Jesus is
the Savior.

I passed on to you as of first importance the message
which I in turn had received, that Christ died for our
sins (1 Cor. 15:3). When we were still sinners, Christ
died for us (Rom. 5:8). Christ Jesus has delivered me
from the Law which entices me to sin and leads to death
(Rom. 8:2).The Lord Jesus Christ sacrificed himself for

our sins that he might deliver us from this present wicked world (Gal. 1:4). In him we have the remission of our sins (Eph. 1:7; Col. 1:14). Trustworthy and deserving of wholehearted acceptance is the saying, "Christ Jesus came into the world to save sinners" (1 Tim. 1:15).

The entire Epistle to the Roman reveals or manifests (2:17, 3:21) God's plan of salvation and underlines its singular appropriateness: God decided to grant pardon and salvation to all men who believe in the proclamation of the Gospel. This is nothing other than the manifestation of the grace of the Father in Jesus Christ. From all eternity, in fact, God, desiring to manifest His goodness, planned this merciful intervention in favor of humanity; this is His "eternally established decree" (Eph. 3:11; Col. 1:26), the "mystery of his will" (Eph. 1:9) that determines the true Christian meaning of history:

> God, who is rich in mercy, was moved by the intense love with which he loved us, and when we were dead by reason of our transgressions, he made us live with the life of Christ. By grace you have been saved . . . It is the gift of God; it is not the result of anything you did (Eph. 2:4–8). The grace of God, which is the means of salvation for all men, has made its appearance and instructed us to reject irreligion and worldly lusts and to live prudent, just, and religious lives in this world, while we await the realization of our blessed hope, the brilliant coming of our great God and Savior Jesus Christ (Tit.

2:11–13). When the goodness and the love of God our
Savior toward all mankind appeared, then, not because of
deeds we ourselves had done in a state of holiness, but in
virtue of his mercy, he saved us through the bath in
which the Holy Spirit regenerates and renews us. This
Spirit God has richly poured out on us through Jesus
Christ our Savior, in order that, made holy by his grace,
we may in hope become heirs of life everlasting (Tit. 3:
4–7; cf. 2 Tim. 1:9).

Each of these texts shows that infinite mercy reached
down to the moral misery of man and that salvation came
through the free love of God. Because the fall of creatures
was utter and irreparable, God intervened in order to show
His glory, that is, His true nature, which is all benignity.
It is true that God can always draw good from evil, but
salvation should not be conceived as a work of wisdom
repairing an accidental disaster in creation. It is the
accomplishment of a will that is supremely merciful as
well as all-comprehending, and which takes complete
initiative in its interventions. Now, the divine decree conceived this prodigious thing: "to assemble all men in
unbelief, that he might have mercy on them all" (Rom.
11:32; cf. Gal. 3:22). "The greater the offense became, so
much the more has grace increased" (Rom. 5:20).

The secret of the divine plan is, in a word, grace. By
the word grace, biblical language designates both the
prevenient and generous love of God and His completely

free gift. When we say that God gives His grace, we understand that He takes the initiative in granting favors. When He shows mercy, it is His goodness pardoning sinners. All His kindnesses are graces because they are granted through His love, which has an inexhaustible capacity for giving. Since an economy or a reign of grace succeeded a reign of sin (Rom. 5:21), the life of man is now dependent upon the assistance and mercy of God (2 Cor. 6:2, 12:9). Life can be explained only with reference to this redeeming love, which is always active in order to save sinners and which maintains them in a personal relationship with God. For St. Paul, grace is not a thing; it is God Himself, living and giving Himself; or, if one prefers, it is His relationship of charity and generosity with men. The superabundant gifts of salvation (2 Cor. 9:14)—from the intelligence and the conquering strength of St. Paul (2 Tim. 2:15),[13] to the Christian virtues (Gal. 1:15; Phil. 1:29)—can henceforth be called grace (2 Cor. 9:14), "for it is God who of his good pleasure accomplishes in you both the will and the attainment" (2:13).

It would be impossible to state more clearly that at the origin of our being as Christians, men saved and redeemed, there is pure gratuitousness. It is not a question of justice, since justice consists in an exchange wherein each one brings what is his own. From God to us there could be no question of justice, for in the beginning we did not even exist. Therefore, we have contributed noth-

ing of our own: *quis prior dedit illi?* Everything has come
from God. There is no possibility of exchange, but only
of pure gift. Gratuitousness, in reality, is the very nature
of the love of charity. As justice considers what is due, so
love is pure charity only when it is spontaneous and free.
In the divine plan, love is the source of everything. The
first meaning of the word *grace* is precisely gratuitousness,
gratia gratis.

It is not superfluous to insist on this point. Because
God wishes to save all men and because our Lord did indeed die for the salvation of the human race (1 Tim. 2:
5–6), sometimes grace is treated as a sort of gift made
once and for all to all men, so that it would be in the
power of each one to draw on it by means of good will.
It is true that the efficacy of the redemption is universal;
but grace, a love, can be given to each one only by a free
and unforeseeable initiative of God the Father. To those
who have not received it, God owes nothing; for their sins
are as so many obstacles to grace; and who is without sin
among the sons and daughters of Adam? The prophet
Osee declared: "Destruction is thy own, O Israel; thy
help is only in me" (13:9). Here we reach the heart of
the inviolable divine liberty. God loves whom He wishes,
and He has His preferences. The thought of God's love
for the elect, for those He has preferred, is overwhelm-
ing. Grace is freely and lovingly given to each one of those
who receive it; it is an effusion of God's goodness. "They

are sanctified freely by his grace" (Rom. 3:24; cf. Rom. 11:6).

Since this is true, the object of Christian faith is to believe in the love of God who pardons sin and "makes all things work together for the good of those who love him" (Rom. 8:28).

> Those whom he has predestined, he has called; and those whom he has called, he has sanctified, and those whom he has sanctified, he has glorified. What shall we conclude after that? If God is for us, who is against us? He who has not spared even his own Son but has delivered him for us all, how can he fail to grant us all other blessings with him? Who shall make accusations against the elect of God? It is God who sanctifies! Who shall condemn? It is Christ Jesus who died, yes, and who rose again, who is at the right hand of God, who also intercedes for us! Who shall separate us from Christ's love for us? Shall tribulation, or distress, or persecution, or hunger, or nakedness, or danger, or the sword? . . . But in all those things we are more than victorious through him who has loved us. I am sure that neither death, nor life, nor angels, nor principalities, nor things present, nor things to come, nor powers, nor height, nor depth, nor any other creature can separate us from God's love for us, which is in Christ Jesus our Lord (Rom. 8:30–39).

For St. Paul's contemporaries, the revelation of this divine charity, all-providential in succoring man's absolute and total misery, aroused the most vibrant and daring *hope*. Far from thinking that everything was lost, the converts to Christianity, who knew the gift of God and possessed it, were assured of triumph. Not only was salvation possible, but sinners were loved! They were able to enjoy divine intimacy even on earth and to approach the throne of grace in all confidence.[14] The pessimism of contemporary paganism was thus replaced by a reasoned and unalterable optimism, based on faith and confidence and on an unshakable certitude: God loves men; He wills their happiness. In Christ He opens the way for them and sets everything to work for the realization of His plan of salvation.

> God leads us in triumphal procession in Christ (2 Cor. 2:14; cf. Col. 2:15). He is able beyond all limits to accomplish immeasurably more than we ask or conceive (Eph. 3:20). God will, in Christ Jesus, gloriously supply your needs in keeping with his riches (Phil. 4:19).

"Superabundance" is the invariable quality of grace or of charity infused by God (1 Thess. 3:12; Rom. 5:20, 2 Cor. 9:14; Eph. 2:7; 1 Tim. 1:14). The divine power accomplishes all our yearning for moral goodness (2 Thess. 1:11).

> (The faithful must know) what is the surpassing greatness of his power toward us believers, . . . the might of this power was shown when he raised Christ from the dead (Eph. 1:19–20). "My grace is sufficient for

> you, for my power is made perfectly evident in your
> weakness." Gladly, therefore, will I boast of my infirmi-
> ties, that the power of Christ may spread a sheltering
> cover over me. For this reason I take delight, for Christ's
> sake, in infirmities, in insults, in hardships, in persecu-
> tions, in distresses. For when I am weak, then I am
> strong (2 Cor. 12:9–10).

Consequently, the Christian life, even in the worst
trials, is lived in an atmosphere of confidence and mag-
nanimity. Since "God makes everything work together for
the good of those who love him," and since "grace is
superabundant," and "we are filled with the fulness of
God," we are conquerors, able to do all in him who
strengthens us (Phil. 4:13).

But our essential reaction in the face of divine goodness, the one which will be the inspiring force of our
moral life, is clearly that of *gratitude*.

> Give thanks joyfully to the Father. He it is who has
> qualified you for a share in the lot of the saints in the
> light, and who has rescued us from the power of dark-
> ness and transferred us into the kingdom of his beloved
> Son, in whom we have our redemption, the remission
> of our sins (Col. 1:12–14).

Gratitude, according to St. Paul, is not an interior sentiment, or even an eminent form of prayer, it is the permanent attitude of a sinful creature who has been mercifully
saved, who knows that he is the object of an infinite love,

and who receives this love, lives by it, and sings its praises.[15] The natural law requires a man to repay his creditor; it is a matter of strict justice. But the response made by Christians to their signal benefactor is spontaneous and free. Indeed, the nuance proper to the charity of Christians is that it is filial. The Father who first loved them has given all; His sons should give back all in a fervent cult of praise. To love God is nothing else than to cling to Him with our whole being, out of gratitude for all He has bestowed on us (cf. 1 Cor. 2:12). Christians take what is most vital and poignant in the sentiment of owing everything to someone who has loved them and showered them with gifts and transport this in an unlimited way to their relations with God. Their charity is a perpetual canticle of thanksgiving to the Holy Trinity: "Thanks be to God for his unutterable gift" (2 Cor. 9:15).

This disposition of soul is so religious and so profound that it is impossible for it not to take the form of worship, praise, and sacrifice: "Whatever you do or say, let it be always in the name of the Lord Jesus, while you give thanks to God the Father through him" (Col. 3:17). St. Paul consecrates the first eleven chapters of his Epistle to the Romans to a description of the mystery of salvation. He shows that all men are sinners and would normally be objects of the divine anger; that the greater the offense became, however, so much the more did grace increase; and that God, being merciful to all, gives His grace and lavishes His love. St. Paul then considers, in the following chapters, what return the Christian should make for this divine love. He presents the virtues to be practiced, obedience, humility, charity, etc., as so many forms of gratitude toward God, as a consecration and an offering of thanksgiving. "I exhort you, therefore, brothers, in view of the mercies of God, to offer your bodies as a sacrifice, living, holy, pleasing to God—such as is the worship of mind and soul" (Rom. 12:1). This consecration of ourselves as a thank-offering is the only response possible to the divine kindnesses. From the moment we become aware of the free gift of our salvation, this living out of our gratitude becomes an obligation. The only suitable way to live henceforth is to devote ourselves body and soul, to sacrifice ourselves to the praise and glory of God. Everything, because it comes from God and from His grace, must return to God under the form of gratitude and praise (Eph. 1:6). Just as there is ingratitude in all sin, there is gratitude in every act of virtue. Fidelity to the divine will is nothing other than a long expression of gratitude. Thus, we will make use of grace according to the very end God has assigned it, and of the divine gifts in conformity with the intentions of their author—the glory of God.

Because a religious morality is defined in terms of a relationship with God, who requires men to act in a certain way in order to obey Him, to reach Him, and to be pleasing to Him, Pauline ethics is an unfolding of gratitude: "Before all else I give thanks" (Rom. 1:8).

We give thanks for salvation (2 Cor. 9:15; Col. 1:12), but also for each particular gift (1 Thess. 3:9; 1 Cor. 1:14; 2 Cor. 1:11, 8:16; Phil. 1:3), notably for food (Rom. 14:6; 2 Cor. 9:11; 1 Tim. 4:3–4) and for "everything" (Col. 3:17): "Give thanks to God for everything. Such is, indeed, the will of God for you in Christ Jesus." And it is a matter of permanent gratitude (1 Thess. 5: 17; 2 Thess. 1:3, 2:13; Col. 1:3; Philem. 4). One never ceases being thankful (1 Thess. 2:13; 1 Cor. 1:4; Eph. 1: 16). "Give thanks to God the Father everywhere and for every gift" (Eph. 5:20). We can never thank God enough for all He has done for us, and we must try to outdo ourselves in gratitude. "May grace profusely granted lead, for God's glory, to profuse thanksgiving" (2 Cor. 4:15; cf. Col. 2:7).

Thus, life on earth is an apprenticeship and a beginning of life in heaven: *Misericordias Domini in aeternum cantabo!*

CHAPTER 3

In Christ Jesus

GRATITUDE IS CLEARLY THE DOMINANT INSPIRATION OF the moral life. This being true, we must determine how Christians are to express their gratitude to God and to live their lives in charity before Him. The all-inclusive response of St. Paul is: *in Christ Jesus.* It is in terms of His Son that God the Father conceived and accomplished all things:

> God, who is rich in mercy, was moved by the intense love with which he loved us, and when we were dead by reason of our transgressions, he made us live with the life of Christ. By grace you have been saved. Together with Christ Jesus and in him, he raised us up and enthroned us in the heavenly realm that in Christ Jesus he might show throughout the ages to come the overflowing riches of his grace springing from his goodness to us (Eph. 2:4–7).

Since it is in Christ that God, out of love for us, conceived and executed His plan of salvation, it is clear that no supernatural reality can exist or can even be thought of apart from Christ. It is in Christ that God chooses and predestines His elect (Eph. 1:4, 5, 11), that He manifests His grace (Tit. 2:11, 3:4), that He communicates His charity (Rom. 8:35–39) and peace (Phil. 4:7), liberty (Gal. 2:4) and light (Eph. 5:8–14), knowledge (Eph. 4:21) and strength (Eph. 6:10).

They are sanctified freely by his grace through the redemption which is in Christ Jesus. God has publicly exhibited him as a means of expiation available to all through the shedding of his blood (Rom. 3:24–25; cf. Gal. 3:13). All this comes from the action of God, who has reconciled us to himself through Christ. . . . God reconciled the world to himself in Christ (2 Cor. 5:18–19; Eph. 2:16). God proves his love for us, because, when we were still sinners, Christ died for us. Much more now that we are sanctified by his blood shall we be saved through him from God's avenging justice. Surely, if when we were enemies we were reconciled to God by the death of his Son, much more, once we are reconciled, shall we be saved by his life (Rom. 5:8–10).

Not only does God give everything through Christ; He receives only what is united to Christ, what passes through Christ, and what comes from Christ. There is, then, only one moral problem for the Christian: participation or union with Christ, in whom he possesses all the treasures of salvation and by whom alone he rejoins God. "From him comes your union in Christ Jesus, who has become for us God-given wisdom and holiness and sanctification and redemption" (1 Cor. 1:30; cf. 6:11). For the converts of St. Paul's day who, humanly speaking, were without reputation or power, who literally "did not exist," this was a prodigious enrichment (1 Cor. 1:28). By means of Christ they passed from nonbeing to being. Supernaturally, they did not exist apart from Him!

St. Paul coined the expression "in Christ," which he

uses more than one hundred sixty times. What precisely does it mean? First of all, it must be emphasized that he is speaking not of the Christ *according to the flesh* (Rom. 1:3–4; 1 Tim. 3:16), but of the risen Christ, living now in heaven, of Him whom the primitive Church described as the *Christ Spirit*, the Lord possessing in its fullness the divine mode of being (2 Cor. 3:17). The heavenly Christ is "spiritual" (1 Cor. 15:45–49). Sharing the same nature and the same attributes of power and glory as the Father, Christ is able to endow His disciples with life and make them divine, "according to his spirit of sanctity." Therefore, from the moment he believes, the Christian is defined as one united to the glorious Christ:

> Moses writes that the man who realizes that holy living which is required by the Law shall find life by it. But the sanctification that comes of faith says, "Do not say in your heart: Who shall ascend into heaven?' (that is, to bring Christ down); or "Who shall descend into the abyss?" (that is, to bring Christ up from the dead). But what does Scripture say? "The message is near you, on your lips and in your heart" (that is, the message of faith which we preach). For if you confess with your lips that *Jesus is the Lord*, and believe in your heart that *God raised him from the dead*, you shall be saved. Because with the heart a man believes and attains holiness, and with the lips profession of faith is made and salvation secured (Rom. 10:5–10). Christ dwells through faith in your hearts (Eph. 3:17).

But how are we to understand this vital relationship? To call it mystical explains nothing, for mystical means merely secret. We gain little in precision by, as it were, localizing the Christian "in Christ," implying that he lives in the atmosphere of Christ and under His influence, for this is to treat the bond with Christ in terms of space or place, when in reality it is a question of two persons who are in each other's presence and who communicate with each other. It is true that the relationship of love between two persons makes it possible for lovers to be always united, in that the one loved lives in the one who loves. But this union remains on the moral and even metaphorical level; whereas the union of Christ and the Christian takes place on the level of being. To explain this absolutely unique case, St. Paul had to coin a new phrase.

In designating the Christian as a "being in Christ," thus directly excluding the notion of fusion or absorption, St. Paul presents much more than a psychological relationship of knowledge and love. He describes a union that is personal, a communion that is reciprocal; or better, an organic and living relationship, a union of life that is the result of our incorporation into Christ. He declares explicitly that we have been grafted onto Christ and implanted in Him (Rom. 6:5), so that we constitute but one being with Him. "All of you who have come to Christ by baptism have clothed yourself with Christ. No longer is there Jew or Greek; no longer is there slave or freeman; no longer is there male or female. You are all one in Christ Jesus" (Gal. 3:27–28). Even though the differences of race, sex, and social condition subsist, each Christian, in his religious being, is *incorporated* into the Lord, becoming but *one in Him* and *with Him*; just as, in the words of our Lord, the branch is a part of the vine (Jn. 15:1).

"To be in Christ Jesus" expresses not so much a bond between the faithful and their Savior, which remains extrinsic to those it unites, as an existential notion, conveying the idea of a "Christian being." Just as every creature is completely dependent upon his Creator and has being only in this "relationship," so the Christian exists supernaturally only in his relationship to Christ. Somewhat like a limb that has life only when it is attached to a body and to the degree in which it receives a vital influx from the head and heart (1 Cor. 6:15), a Christian has his being of grace through dependence on Christ. One who receives everything he is from another cannot be conceived of apart from this other. In the same way the Christian can be conceived of only in relation to Christ because without Christ he would not exist, that is, supernaturally: "If any man is in Christ, he is a new creation; the old state of things has gone; wonderful to tell, it has been made over, absolutely new!" (2 Cor. 5:17).

And so, to be Christian means to be in Christ, for

Christ, and by Christ. Tradition has understood this in the most realistic sense possible. The Syriac version translated Heb. 3:4—"participants of Christ"—as "those mixed with Christ," and St. John Chrysostom comments even more forcefully: "We form but one with him. . . . We are consubstantial with Christ."[16] At the opposite pole from the pagan, who is a "being in the flesh," the Christian is essentially "a man in Christ" (2 Cor. 12:12). Just as he is described as *deified* by the grace of the Father, or *spiritualized* by the action of the Holy Spirit, we ought to speak of him as *Christified*, to explain his being and his existence "in Christ." St. Athanasius spoke of the Christian as "wordified," that is, made the Word.[17]

The pagans who were converted by hearing the message of the apostles believed both in the infinite love of God and in the resurrection and omnipotence of Christ: "He whom God raised to life did not see decay" (Acts 13:37; cf. Rom. 10:9; 1 Thess. 1:9–10). The *faith* that saves is our belief in Christ (Rom. 3:26; 1 Thess. 4:14), the glorious Savior (2 Thess. 2:14) and the Son of God (Acts 9:20, 13:33), from whom we receive life (1 Thess. 5:10; Eph. 2:5). The convert's act of faith procured for him the pardon of his sins and the purification of his soul. But it was at his baptism, the regeneration and renewal of his very being (Tit. 3:4–7), that he was incorporated into Christ and that he participated fully in His grace. In fact, baptism unites the Christian so completely to his

Savior that not only does he live "in Christ" and in union with Him, but his life is henceforth that of Christ Himself living in him. Christ died and rose again, and the baptized person shares in this death and resurrection. He relives them for himself, and renews them so truly that it can be said that he dies and is buried with Christ, and then rises, lives again, and reigns with Christ.

> Do you not know that all of us who have been baptized into union with Christ Jesus have been baptized into union with his death? Yes, we were buried in death with him by means of baptism, in order that, just as Christ was raised from the dead by the glorious power of the Father, so we also may conduct ourselves by a new principle of life (Rom. 6:3–4).

The consequence is evident. The Christian life—a symbiosis with the Lord, to borrow a term from biology (Rom. 6:8; Col. 2:13)—will be nothing other than the living and the putting into effect of this baptismal grace, a continuous, progressive death to sin and a life of renewal and victory:

> We carry about with us in our bodies at all times Jesus' condemnation to death, so that in these same bodies of ours the living power of Jesus may become evident (2 Cor. 4:10–11). Buried with him by baptism, you also rose with him by your faith in the power of God who raised him from the dead (Col. 2:12).

This double rhythm of the crucifixion and resurrection of the Savior, impressed like stigmata on the very being of the Christian (Gal. 6:17), marks his whole existence. What he has acquired once and for all ontologically, he must develop and perfect psychologically and morally:

> Since we have grown to be one with him through a death like his, we shall also be one with him by a resurrection like his. We know that our old self has been crucified with him, in order that the body enslaved to sin may be reduced to impotence, and we may no longer be slaves to sin; for he who is dead is once and for all quit of sin. But if we have died with Christ, we believe that we shall also live with him, since we know that Christ, having risen from the dead, will die no more; death shall no longer have dominion over him. The death that he died was a death to sin once for all, but the life that he lives is a life for God. Thus you too must consider yourselves dead to sin, but alive to God in Jesus Christ. Do not then let sin reign in your mortal body so as to obey its lusts. And do not go on offering your members to sin as instruments of iniquity, but once for all dedicate yourselves to God as men that have come to life from the dead, and your members as instruments of holiness for God; for sin shall not have dominion over you, since you are not the subjects of the Law but of grace (Rom. 6:5–14).

Such is the end to strive for. The baptized Christian is no longer subject to the demands of the flesh, itself a slave of the reign of sin, but rather to Christ: "Those who belong to Christ have crucified their flesh with its passionate cravings" (Gal. 5:24). A transfer of property and authority has taken place: "All of you who have come to Christ by baptism have clothed yourself with Christ. . . . You are Christ's" (Gal. 3:27, 29; Rom. 13: 14). So true is this transfer that the converts of St. Paul's day found themselves in a state of irreconcilable opposition toward the world; they were about to live in conditions completely different from those that preceded their conversion. Won by Christ and paid for by Christ—the contract of sale in Greek antiquity was sealed by the payment of the price—they would henceforth live for Christ: "Our Lord Jesus Christ died for us in order that we might find life in union with him" (1 Thess. 5:10).

> Love for Christ impels us. We have come to the conclusion that since one died for all, therefore all died, and that Christ died for all, in order that they who are alive may live no longer for themselves, but for him who died for them and rose again (2 Cor. 5:14–15). None of us lives for himself, and none dies for himself. If we live, we live for the Lord, and if we die, we die for the Lord. Whether we live or whether we die, we are the Lord's. To this end Christ died and lived, that he might be Lord both of the dead and of the living (Rom. 14:7–9).

St. Paul's insistence in reminding Christians that they no longer belong to themselves but are become the property of Christ is based first of all on their profession of faith at baptism, when they proclaimed: "Jesus is the one Lord" (1 Cor. 8:6); secondly, it is based on this sentence of our Lord: "A man cannot be the slave of two masters. He will either hate the one and love the other, or, at least, be attentive to the one and neglectful of the other" (Matt. 6:24); and finally, on the contemporary custom of emancipating slaves under the form of a sale to divinity. Slaves could free themselves by paying their owners a sum of money that they had laboriously earned. Many masters, however, after having received the "ransom," kept their slaves in servitude. From this abuse arose the practice of paying money to the treasury of the god Apollo, who would then "ransom" the slave from his master and guarantee him protection against every evil. For example, a "receipt" is extant that reads: "Cleon, son of Cleoxenos, sold to Pythian Apollo a male body (the customary designation of a slave), bearing the name Istiacos, a Syrian, for the price of four minas, on the condition that Istiacos be free and that no one be permitted to touch him for the rest of his life." The purpose of this bill of sale was to transfer the right of ownership. As soon as the stipulated sum was paid, the slave ceased to belong to his former owner; redeemed by the god he became free and was henceforth his own master. It is explicitly stated that at no time could he be seized by anyone, that he could do what he wished and live where he wished for the rest of his life.

For St. Paul, Christ had poured forth His blood in ransom to liberate the slaves of sin. His disciples are "bought at a price" (1 Cor. 6:20), and therefore are free. So true is this that we can substitute for the word "redemption," which is no longer meaningful, the word "liberation," so significant to contemporary ears. There is this difference, however, between the man ransomed by Apollo and the man ransomed by Christ. The former could henceforth "do what he wanted," according to the terms of the contract; the latter belongs body and soul to his Savior. Freed from sin, he becomes the slave of Christ, whom he recognizes as his new Master. Because of his desire to live in sanctity, he submits voluntarily and joyfully to this yoke which is sweet and light: "He who was called in the Lord, while he was a slave, has become a freedman of the Lord, just as he who was called while he was a freedman has become a slave of Christ. You have been bought with a price! Do not enslave yourselves to men" (1 Cor. 7:22–23).

Expressive though they are, juridical metaphors are insufficient when it comes to plumbing the depth of the "mystery of Christ," of explaining how the Christian, who is now the property of his "Redeemer," has no existence and no life apart from Him. Therefore, St. Paul coins neologisms and uses them over and over to convey the truth that no matter what his state of life or what his work, the Christian is not only united to Christ, but lives his life in and with Christ, *cum Christo.* Just as he suffers and dies with Christ, he lives with Christ, grows with Christ, is conformed to Christ; a co-heir with Christ, he is glorified and enthroned with Christ and reigns with him. His very being is defined in terms of a Person, and so, too, is his life: "Your life is hidden with Christ in God" (Col. 3:3).

What most clearly characterizes this "new man" (Eph. 2:15, 4:24) or "new creature" (2 Cor. 5:17; Gal. 6:15) is the loss of his autonomy. Since he is formed by insertion into Christ and by belonging to the Lord (Gal. 3:29), the Christian could not possibly be the source of his own life or the guide of his own actions. Apart from the fact that he is *in* Christ and lives *with* Christ, it is Christ who, living in him, makes him live: "With Christ I am nailed to the cross. *It is now no longer I that live, but Christ lives in me.* The life that I now live in this body, I live by [the union of] faith in the Son of God who loved me and sacrificed himself for me" (Gal. 2:19–20.)

Here we reach the heart of Pauline ethics: the moral life is a prolongation, an extension, an unfolding of the life of Christ in His disciples. The "rule of life" of the Christian is to *conform* his thought and his conduct to

Christ, who is the perfect model, and thus to become ever more perfectly incorporated into Him. This is the express will of God, the reason for the creation of the world and the predestination of the faithful. Indeed, just as God established His Son as center of the plan of salvation and head of the universe, "gathering all creation both in heaven and on earth under one head, Christ" (Eph. 1:10, 20–23, 2:14–22, 4:15), so He sees and loves the elect only in Christ. "Those whom he has foreknown he has also predestined to be conformed to the image of his Son, so that this Son should be the first-born among many brothers."[18]

Every Christian is *called* to be a sharer in the glory of the Son of God, and, in so doing, to contribute to this glory. The risen Lord is to be surrounded in heaven by the multitude of men whom He has saved. More precisely, Christians resemble the glorious Christ as the younger members of a family resemble their elder brother (Heb. 2:10–12). Christians are authentic children of God even here on earth, possessing by grace the same divine nature as their Father in heaven (Eph. 1:5; Gal. 4:5). If Christ is the Son of God by nature, the faithful are sons by adoption and by an adoption as real as any generation (Rom. 8:15–17). Now each son resembles his Father. Jesus is the exact reproduction, "the radiant reflection of God's glory and the express image of his nature" (Heb. 1:3); and the adopted sons must try to be "imitators of

God, as his very dear children" (Eph. 5:1). But because God is invisible and because it would be impossible to reproduce a model that one has never contemplated, it is the image of the Father in Christ that Christians must make their own. St. Paul presents himself as an example to his disciples in this way: "Become imitators of me as I am of Christ" (1 Cor. 4:16; cf. 11:1, 1 Thess. 1:6).

The orientation of life of the sons of God is clear beyond all doubt. Since they have become the property of Christ by the baptismal rite, their consecration must be so total that they will live and die only for their Lord. United to Christ as a member is to its body, they must try to assimilate this new life, which is the life of Christ Himself. The moral life is nothing other than the pursuit of an ever more profound assimilation, an ever more total conformity. *Mimesis*, the Greek word used in the above text, signifies "reproduction" and "representation." Consequently, as one becomes more fully the possession of the Lord, the transformation into His image becomes a more perfect resemblance to Him, more exact and manifest. The true Christian life, which comes from the glorious, immanent Christ—*Christus in vobis* (2 Cor. 13:5; Eph. 3:17; Col. 1:27)—is a gradual metamorphosis, by means of which the copy becomes each day an ever more exact likeness of the model: "All of us, reflecting as in a mirror the Lord's glory, are being transformed into his very image from one degree of splendor to another, such as comes from the Lord who is the spirit" (2 Cor. 3:18).

We are *true* Christians in the measure that the traits of the Lord can be discerned in us: *Christianus alter Christus!* It goes without saying that the similarity can never be total. But since our predestination, our very reason for being, is to be an "image" of the well-beloved Son, then we must pursue throughout our lives this quest for a more complete resemblance "until we all attain to unity in faith and deep knowledge of the Son of God. Thus we attain to perfect manhood, to the mature proportions that befit Christ's fullness" (Eph. 4:13). The glorious resurrection of the body will bring the ultimate completion of this "configuration": "Just as we have borne the likeness of the man of dust [Adam], so shall we bear the likeness of the Heavenly One [Jesus]" (1 Cor. 15:49).

This law of the imitation of Christ is so truly the unique moral rule of Christianity that it applies to all ages, all conditions, and all stages of life:

> Strip off the old self with its deeds and put on the new, which is being progressively remodeled after the image of its Creator and brought to deep knowledge. Here there is no Gentile, no Jew, no circumcised, no uncircumcised, no barbarian, no Scythian, no slave, no free man, but Christ is everything in each of us (Col. 3:9–11; cf. Gal. 3:28).

Men or women, rich or poor, great or small, the faithful

are members of the divine family and they conduct themselves according to the principles of their heavenly Father, as they see them realized in Christ.

It is not that Christians must reproduce the deeds and accomplishments of the Savior materially, and thus superficially, but they must adopt His manner of thinking and judging (1 Cor. 2:16), be inspired with His sentiments, copy His virtues, imitate His charity, and have the same filial piety toward the Father. The golden rule is: *To have in oneself the same sentiments which were in Christ Jesus* (Rom. 15:5; Phil. 2:5). It is not a question of practicing some particular virtue, of reforming oneself, of controlling one's acts by reason, or of conducting oneself as a man of principle, but of acting as Christ would act, of forming judgments *analogous* to His, of loving with the same generosity and the same delicacy as He would love, of being patient and humble as He would be, since, once again, it is Christ in person who lives in the Christian and gives him his life. Efficient causality produces in him whom it moves a formal or "conformed" resemblance.

Consequently, whatever the particular act in question may be, it must be adjusted to the thought and the charity of Christ. For example, when St. Paul has to recall the Romans or the Philippians to humility, he reminds them that "Christ did not please himself" (Rom. 15:3), that they should

be of the same mind as Christ Jesus, who, though he is

by nature God, did not consider his equality with God a condition to be clung to, but emptied himself by taking the nature of a slave, fashioned as he was to the likeness of men. . . . He humbled himself and became obedient to death; yes, to the death on the cross (Phil. 2:5–8).

When he seeks to encourage the Corinthians to give generous help to the poor of Jerusalem, he writes: "You know the graciousness of our Lord Jesus Christ. Although he was rich, he became poor for your sakes that by his poverty you might become rich" (2 Cor. 8:9); thus must you act toward one another. When he finds the Ephesians lacking in charity he admonishes them to consider the example of the Lord:

Let all bitter resentment, and passion, and anger, and loud abusive speech, in a word, every kind of malice, be banished from your midst. On the contrary, be kind to one another, and merciful, generously forgiving one another, as also God in Christ has generously forgiven you. Therefore, follow God's example, as his very dear children, and let your conduct be guided by love, as Christ also loved us and delivered himself for us (Eph. 4:31–5:2).

The same exhortation is given to the Colossians:

Therefore, as God's chosen ones, holy and well beloved, clothe yourselves with the sentiments of compassion, kindness, humility, meekness, long-suffering. Bear with one another and forgive whatever grievances you have

against each other. Just as the Lord has forgiven you, so
you must forgive (Col. 3:12–13).

The delicacy and devotedness of fraternal charity are
inspired by the example of Christ: "Welcome one another cordially, even as Christ has welcomed you to himself for the glory of God" (Rom. 15:7). Any division
among Christians is the same as dismembering Christ,
for Christ, living in each one of them, has made of them
one body (1 Cor. 1:12–13, 12:12). "You are all one in
Christ Jesus" (Gal. 3:28). Out of foolish vanity the Corinthians have scandalized a brother who is weak and have
thus made him subject to destruction; how can they forget that Christ died for this brother (1 Cor. 8:11–13;
cf. Rom. 14:15)? It is inconceivable that a lie should
come from the lips of a disciple of Christ who was veracity
itself: "The Son of God . . . did not prove to be Yes
and No . . . in him was realized the Yes" (2 Cor. 1:17–
20).

The reason we must keep ourselves pure is that our
bodies are the members of Christ; to sin against one's
body is to impair the consecration that unites it to the
Lord (1 Cor. 6:15–18). Even spouses are united in the
Lord (1 Cor. 7:39, 11:11); marriage can be lived in a
Christian way only if the husband and wife love each
other after the manner of Christ who on the cross united
Himself to sinful humanity in order to engender it to
grace:

Let wives be subject to their husbands who are representatives of the Lord, because the husband is head of the wife just as Christ is the head of the Church and also the savior of that body. Thus, just as the Church is subject to Christ, so also let wives be subject to their husbands in all things.

Husbands, love your wives, just as Christ loved the Church, and delivered himself for her, that he might sanctify her by cleansing her in the bath of water with the accompanying word, in order to present to himself the Church in all her glory, devoid of blemish or wrinkle or anything of the kind, but that she may be holy and flawless. Even so ought husbands to love their wives as their own bodies. He who loves his wife, loves himself. Now no one ever hates his own flesh; on the contrary, he nourishes and cherishes it, as Christ does the Church, because we are members of his Body. "For this cause a man shall leave his father and mother, and cling to his wife; and the two shall become one flesh." This is a great mystery—I mean in regard to Christ and the Church (Eph. 5:22–32).

It is precisely in this reproduction of the union of Christ and the Church that marriage has its "significance," its *sacramental* value. Conjugal union symbolizes and "imitates" the Savior's total gift of self to His beloved spouse. The love of marriage is a love of union and fecundity; it is "Christianized" by the *imitation* of the charity by which Christ is united to men and regenerates them.

There is no act, no matter how slight, which the Christian is not able to accomplish in the spirit of Jesus Christ. He will speak and he will say the truth in Christ (Rom. 9:1; Eph. 4:21), just as St. Paul exhorted and commanded in the Lord (1 Thess. 4:1; 2 Thess. 3:6, 12), just as he had confidence or was proud in him (1 Cor. 1:31; Gal. 5:10). The Christian, rooted and established in the Lord, will conduct himself in conformity with what he has learned from him (Col. 2:6). To hold fast and to persevere is possible only in him (1 Thess. 3:8; Phil. 4:1). Therefore, the Christian will receive his brothers (Rom. 16:2) and will greet them in the Lord (1 Cor. 16:19; Rom. 16:22). Children will obey, just as a wife will be subject, in the Lord (Eph. 6:1; Col. 3:18).

Likewise, if we struggle and toil, our struggle and toil will have value only in the Lord (Rom. 16:12) and in the fact that we experience the sufferings of Christ Himself (2 Cor. 1:5). Prisoners in the Lord (Eph. 4:1; Philem. 23) and weak in Christ (2 Cor. 13:4), we are united to Him in a communion of sacrifice, and thus we participate in His death (Phil. 3:10; Col. 1:24); we endure all things with His patience (2 Thess. 3:5). In the same way, we are filled with joy (Phil. 3:1, 4:10), with courage (Rom. 15:17; 1 Cor. 15:31; Phil. 3:3), and with strength in Christ (Eph. 6:10); we possess and reproduce His kind-

ness and gentleness (2 Cor. 10:1), His truth (2 Cor. 11:
10), His exceedingly tender mercy (Phil. 1:8), and His
peace: "Let the ruling principle of your hearts be the
peace of Christ" (Col. 3:15; Phil. 4:7). The phrase "in
the Lord" or "in Christ" could often be translated "in
a Christian manner," which expresses the mode of thinking, of loving, and of acting, proper to "those who are of
Christ."

St. Paul calls this imitation of Christ the accomplishment of the Law of Christ (Gal. 6:2), or again his "teach-
ings and methods," rules of life which he taught everywhere, to every congregation (1 Cor. 4:17), and by means
of which they now walk according to the Lord (Rom.
15:5; 2 Cor. 11:17; Col. 2:8). This ethic is simply the
consequence of the union of being and life with Christ.
As one is, so he lives, thinks, and loves. Little by little,
the life of Christ appears in our bodies (2 Cor. 5:10),
since Christians, in effacing themselves, only manifest
more clearly what they are interiorly: other Christs. The
resemblance is so exact that in St. Paul's hymn to charity
(1 Cor. 13:4–8), where he presents his ideal of life for
each Christian, we can, by replacing the word *charity*
with the word *Christ*, have a portrait of the Savior:
"Christ is long-suffering; Christ is kind; he is not self-
seeking; he takes no note of injury; always he is ready to
make allowances, always to be patient. . . ."

Each baptized person is called to say again, with the

assurance of St. Paul: "For me to live means Christ" (Phil. 1:21). To make this notion of life precise, one would expect a verb here or some term expressing an action or a state, but St. Paul names a Person, who represents to him his all: the Lord! This mode of expression is truly a creation inspired by love, but also by genius, since St. Paul transfers to the new religion the great principle of ethics in antiquity: γένοιο οἷος εἶ, *Become what you are!* St. Thomas Aquinas later expressed in the words: *Viventibus, vivere est esse.*

The Spirit says:

> Awake, sleeper,
> And arise from the dead,
> And Christ will give you light (Eph. 5:14).

CHAPTER 4

By the Holy Spirit

How can christians live "in christ jesus" and imitate His virtues, especially His charity? How can they serve God alone, joyfully expressing their gratitude to Him all day long and seeking only His glory? How can they respond worthily to their vocation (2 Thess. 1:11; Eph. 4:1), keep themselves spotless in the midst of an evil world, triumph over sin and Satan, and become ever more holy? To live the Christian morality is absolutely impossible for a man who admits from his own experience: I am carnal; no good dwells in me; evil is ready at hand; to wish is within my power, but I do not find the strength to accomplish what is good (Rom. 7:14, 18, 21). "To live in Christ Jesus" is made possible because the the Holy Spirit "comes to help our weakness" (8:26).

Few realities are as foreign to modern minds as that of the biblical *spirit*. For us, the word "spirit" signifies spirituality, soul, nonmateriality, intelligence; whereas the Hebrew word, meaning breath, and especially vital breath, suggests the idea of strength, power, and accomplishment. In biblical terminology, a "holy spirit" is a gift of God that communicates a new energy; while the soul is the principle of natural life, the spirit is the principle of all religious knowledge and of the virtues; it is a participation in the very life of God. In our own day, we call this participation "sanctifying grace." Initially, it is the person of the "Holy Spirit," who

creates in us all the faculties and works of the Christian
life.

At the moment of his adoption as a son of God, the
Christian receives the Holy Spirit. When St. Paul ar-
rived at Damascus after his conversion by Christ,
Ananias, a disciple of the first hour, declared to him:
"The Lord has sent me . . . , that you may receive your
sight and be filled with the Holy Spirit" (Acts 9:17).
And at Ephesus, when he met some disciples of John
the Baptist, who believed in Christ the Savior but were
not yet baptized, he asked them: "Did you receive the
Holy Spirit when you became believers?" (Acts 19:2).
The Holy Spirit is the specific gift (Rom. 5:5) that
God grants to each baptized person at the intercession
of his Son (cf. Jn. 14:16, 26). He is the Spirit of the
risen Christ by whose life His members live:

> You are not sensual but spiritual, if the Spirit of God
> really dwells in you, whereas no one who is deprived
> of the Spirit of Christ belongs to Christ. But if Christ
> is in you, the body, it is true, is destined to death be-
> cause of sin, but the spirit has life because of its holi-
> ness. And if the Spirit of him who raised Jesus from
> the dead dwells in you, then he who raised Christ
> Jesus from the dead will also bring to life your mortal
> bodies because of his Spirit who dwells in you (Rom.

8:9–11). God sent the Spirit of his Son into our hearts
(Gal. 4:6). We were all given to drink of a single Spirit
(1 Cor. 12:13).

Molded from clay, the first man became by the
divine breath "a soul having life"; so, too, the new
Adam became, for all his race, "a spirit imparting life"
(1 Cor. 15:45; cf. 2 Cor. 3:17). In the language of the
New Testament, the word "spirit" connotes essentially
life and strength; hence it implies an immanent and
dynamic agent. For example, the archangel announced
to our Lady the birth of Jesus with the words: "The
Holy Spirit will come upon you; the power of the Most
High will overshadow you" (Luke 1:35). When the
Lord promised to send the Holy Spirit to His apostles,
he said: "You shall receive power when the Holy Spirit
comes upon you" (Acts 1:8). Therefore, since the Holy
Spirit is the immediate and constant life-giving principle
of the moral life, it is clear that the Christian is "strengthened with power through the Spirit for the development
of your inner selves" (Eph. 3: 16).

According to St. Paul, the Holy Spirit is much more
than the "gift of God" that sums up all the other gifts
of salvation, more even than the agent of our sanctification, who communicates grace to us and incites us to
virtue. He is the very source of our spiritual life, so

much so that the new morality, contrasting markedly with Israelite morality which was based on the Commandments, is a life that responds to the movement of the Holy Spirit.[19] The new morality is defined as "the law of the Spirit" (Rom. 8:2). This means that we are dependent on the Holy Spirit alone, on His inspiration and on His impulse (Rom. 8:10), and that we act "according to the Spirit" (Rom 8:4; Gal. 5:18). Such is the hallmark of genuine Christians: "Whoever are led by the Spirit of God, they are the sons of God" (Rom. 8:14). In a word, it is because "we render service to God which is new and according to the Spirit" (Rom. 7:6), that the economy of the new Alliance is specifically different from the old.

The relationship of Christians to Christ is similar to a grafting or an incorporation, while their relationship to the Holy Spirit may be compared to an indelible mark stamped by a seal:

> It is God who has established us firmly along with you in communion with Christ, and has anointed us, and stamped us with his seal, and given us the Spirit as the first installment of what is to come (2 Cor. 1:21–22). After you had heard the message of truth, and had believed in it you have been sealed with the promised Holy Spirit, who is the first installment of our inheritance (Eph. 1:13–14). Do not grieve the Holy Spirit of God,

by whom you have been sealed in preparation for the day of redemption (Eph. 4:30).

The Greek word used here is that designating the official stamp or trade-mark which served to authenticate the agreement between contracting parties or to establish the existence of a piece of property. The setting of a seal ratified and confirmed the intention and rights of the owner. For instance, slaves, soldiers, and prisoners of war in antiquity were "marked" in the name of the emperor or of their owners. The seal was also used as a sign of consecration. The emblem of a particular god, worn by certain faithful souls, indicated that they had bound themselves to his service and enrolled themselves in his cult. According to Ezechiel (9:4–6), God had marked His servants with a sign on their foreheads that assured them of salvation and of protection against all evil. Every Christian bears a similar mark (Apoc. 7:3, 9:4, 14:1). Because a baptized person belongs to his Lord, he is consigned to His service; the relationship is sealed by the gift of the Holy Spirit. Thus this new creature, who lives by the Holy Spirit, has within him the sign of his incorporation into the new Alliance, and consequently the assurance of obtaining all its promises. This "seal" of the Spirit is then objectively an infallible guarantee, and subjectively a proof that one is a son of God, beloved of the Father, and freed from the slavery of sin. The seal is, as it were, the first installment of what is to come; for a life dependent upon the movement of the Holy Spirit cannot but assure entrance into heaven, "in view of the day of our final redemption":

> In fact we are certain that when our earthly dwelling, which is but a tent, is destroyed, we have an edifice made by God, a dwelling not made with hands, everlasting in the heavens. And in truth we pine in this present dwelling, yearning to have put over it that dwelling of ours which is from heaven, if indeed we shall be found clothed and not naked. For we who are in this tent sigh under our burden, because we do not wish to be unclothed, but rather clothed over, that what is mortal may be swallowed up by life. Now he who has fashioned us for this very purpose is God, who has given us the Spirit as the first installment of what is to come (2 Cor. 5:1–5).

This vital ascendancy of the Holy Spirit over the Christian dates from the first day of his rebirth in God (Gal. 3:2). It is, in fact, to the Holy Spirit, conjointly with Christ, that the regeneration and renewal of baptism are attributed (Tit. 3:5). "You have been washed clean; you have been sanctified; you have been made holy in the name of our Lord Jesus Christ and in the Spirit of our God" (1 Cor. 6:11). Because the Holy Spirit communicates His divine nature and life to the Christian, making him a son of God and a brother of

Christ, in the most real sense of these terms, He is called "the spirit of filiation." As such, He both establishes between the baptized person and God the relationship of child to Father and guides his moral life so that it is led not in a slave's spirit of indifference or fear but in the spirit of an adopted son: in fidelity, love, and confidence.

In order that those who have been raised to such a noble rank may fulfill their obligations and be completely at ease living "in the presence of God in charity" (Eph. 1:4), a complete education is necessary, which can only be given by the Holy Spirit in person. He alone can bestow a Christian "mentality" upon these adopted sons, fill them with the thoughts and sentiments of the Father and Son, and suggest to them the attitudes required by such a relationship. First and foremost, the Christian must dare to name the all-holy God: "my Father," and he must have the intimate conviction of being His son:

> Whoever are led by the Spirit of God, they are the sons of God. Now you have not received a spirit of bondage so that you are again in fear, but you have received a spirit of adoption as sons, in virtue of which we cry, "Abba! Father!" The Spirit himself joins his testimony to that of our spirit that we are children of God (Rom. 8:14–16). When the designated period of time had elapsed, God sent his Son, born of a woman,

born in subjection to the Law, in order to redeem those who were in subjection to the Law, that we might receive the adoption. And because you are sons, God sent the Spirit of his Son into your hearts, crying, "Abba, Father." You are, then, no longer a slave but a son; and if a son, an heir also through God's grace (Gal. 4:4–7).

These texts, and many others besides, testify that Christians do have an awareness of their new relationship to God, an experience of the presence and the reality of grace. For the Holy Spirit, speaking in their hearts, convincingly persuades them of their authentic sonship. He teaches them to call upon God, their Father, by the name that Christ himself used: *Abba*. Jesus also used this same word when he addressed St. Joseph. The Israelites, in their prayers, said, "*Abi*, my Father"; the word *Abba*, however, is more intimate and familiar, corresponding to our "Papa." And so, when the Christian dares to pronounce such a name, he is not calling upon the loving providence of God the Creator, but more specifically upon the fatherhood by which God has communicated His own nature to him and has called him to the abode of the Holy Trinity: "You are no longer foreigners and guests; no, you are fellow citizens with the saints, and members of God's household" (Eph. 2:19). Still more, it is the Son of God Himself who, through the Holy Spirit, calls upon His Father, uniting Himself to all His brothers in a common prayer. This is the meaning of the words of St. Athanasius:

> Because the Word has assumed our body . . . , it is fitting by reason of the Word which is in us, that God should also be called our Father. For the Spirit of the Word which lives in us through us calls his Father ours. This is also what St. Paul means when he says: "God sent the Spirit of his Son into your hearts, crying, 'Abba, Father!' "[20]

Because Christians have received the Holy Spirit and live according to His light and in His love, their new morality becomes a morality of sonship. They act as befits the sons of such a Father! The wonderful thing is that this divine way of acting is instilled into them from heaven—we are taught by God (1 Thess. 4:9)—and yet that they are so intimately persuaded of this mystery! A morality of the Commandments, even one dictated by sublime motives, imposes a fixed line of action from the outside; but Christians, sons of God, can decide for themselves, supported by a certitude and strength that the Holy Spirit continually infuses into them.

The "spirit" of the man who has been regenerated is the Holy Spirit's place of dwelling and the organ by which he perceives and accepts the Holy Spirit's movements. It is, as it were, his faculty of the divine that enables him to know the will of God (Rom. 12:2) and to apply it to his

daily life: "If we live by the Spirit, let us conduct ourselves by the Spirit" (Gal. 5:25).

The first and in a sense the predominant action of the
Holy Spirit in us is to oppose the flesh and its cravings,
to put to death the deeds of the lower nature (Rom.
8:13), and to triumph over sin which dwells in us (Rom.
7:17):

> I say: conduct yourselves by the Spirit, and you will not
> yield to the cravings of sensuality. The cravings of sen-
> suality are opposed to the Spirit, and the Spirit opposed
> to sensuality. These two are arrayed against each other
> (Gal. 5:16–17). Those who live under the control of
> their lower instincts set their minds on the carnal, but
> those who live under the control of the Spirit set their
> minds on the spiritual. Sensual-mindedness leads to
> death, but spiritual-mindedness leads to life and peace
> (Rom. 8:5–6).

The Epistle to the Galatians contrasts the "actions
prompted by sensuality: fornication, impurity, licentiousness, idolatry, witchcraft, enmity, contention, jeal-
ousy, outbursts of anger, quarrels, factions, schisms, envy,
drunkenness, carousings, and other vices similar to these"
(5:19–21) with the fruits of the Spirit: "love, joy, peace,
long-suffering, affability, goodness, fidelity, gentleness,
self-control" (5:22–23).

The Christian life is a continual tension between the
demands of the flesh and the will of God, between en-

slavement to sin and filial love. The work of the Holy Spirit consists in progressively spiritualizing us; little by little, He makes us pass from one world to the other, purifying us and making us divine. He transforms the sinner into a child of God, the slave and prisoner into a free man, the defeated into the triumphant, the one condemned to death into the one gloriously resurrected (Rom. 8:11).

Thus, the morality of the Holy Spirit can be called a *morality of sanctity*, in the sense that it is a consecration to God: "He who unites himself to the Lord, forms one spirit with him" (1 Cor. 6:16).

> What God wills is your sanctification. He wills that you abstain from immorality (1 Thess. 4:3). God has not called us to uncleanness but to holiness. So, he who rejects these teachings rejects not man but the God who has given you his Holy Spirit (1 Thess. 4:7–8). Do not extinguish the Spirit. . . . have nothing to do with any kind of evil. May God himself, the author of peace, make you perfect in holiness. May every part of your being, spirit, soul and body, be preserved blameless for the day when our Lord Jesus Christ shall come (1 Thess. 5:19–23). As you offered your members to be slaves of uncleanness and iniquity, culminating in utter wickedness, so now offer your members to be slaves of right living, culminating in holiness (Rom. 6:19). The law of the Spirit which directs my life in Christ Jesus has delivered me from the Law which entices me to sin and leads to

death (Rom. 8:2). Let everyone who names the name of the Lord depart from iniquity (2 Tim. 2:19).

By the very fact that he is crucified to the world and purified from sin, the Christian affirms that he belongs body and soul to the Lord and that he lives in dependence on Him alone. Even his submission, which is an act of worship, praises the Lord: "God's temple, which you yourselves are, is holy" (1 Cor. 3:17; cf. 6:19). The moral life is like a sacrifice (Rom. 12:1), "an oblation sanctified by the Holy Spirit" (Rom. 15:16; cf. 2 Cor. 11:2). It is not so much a question of being upright and blameless, producing good works in abundance (Phil. 1:11), as of being "holy and without blemish" (Eph. 1:4). Like the victims chosen for immolation whose integrity made them a sacrifice worthy of God, they should do what "befits saints," that is, act religiously (Rom. 16:2; Eph. 5:3). Such a manner of acting comes from the Holy Spirit (Gal. 5:25): "God has selected you from eternity to be saved through the sanctification which the Spirit effects" (2 Thess. 2:13).

Because Pauline morality is a morality of the Spirit, it is consequently a *morality of liberty.* We have seen how profound was St. Paul's pessimism when he judged humanity apart from Christ; men were slaves to sin and death, to the flesh, to the Law, and to Satan. Salvation presented itself first of all as a liberation from all these enslavements: "There is now no longer any condemnation against those who are in Christ Jesus. For the law of the Spirit which directs your life in Christ Jesus has delivered you from the Law which entices you to sin and leads to death" (Rom. 8:1–2). Deliverance is the distinctive work of the Lord: "The Lord is the spirit, and where this Spirit of the Lord is, there is freedom" (2 Cor. 3:17); and liberty is the hallmark of the Christian vocation: "You have been called to liberty" (Gal. 5:13). By this mark the Church is distinguished from the Synagogue, whose children are born into bondage while "we are children of the free woman" (Gal. 4:31). Liberty is finally the keynote of our moral striving, which is a progressive emancipation and not a forced submission: "Christ has set us free to enjoy freedom" (Gal. 5:1). So true is this that we can affirm: "The Law is not enacted for the just" (1 Tim. 1:9), who are moved by the Holy Spirit.

The finality of these statements shows that the liberty in question is not simply a single virtue or a fruit of the Spirit. It is the Christian life itself in its soul and source, in its most formal aspects: the Holy Spirit and the grace of God. In other words, the moral life of the baptized person, who is in Christ, is not based on a set of precepts. The Christian does not have to observe a law that will be imposed on him from outside, but rather a law of grace, or of Christ dwelling within him (Rom. 6:15; 1 Cor. 9:21; Gal. 6:2). This law, inscribed on his heart of flesh, inspires and directs his spontaneity and fervor from within. It is the liberty of God Himself that reigns in the souls of His children, thanks to the action of the Holy Spirit.

The moral life does not become anarchic because of this; it remains subject to a law, but to a "new law," "the law of the Spirit who gives life." In place of being ruled and directed from without and by another, Christians act spontaneously, that is, freely. They are not constrained, like slaves "under" the yoke of a law; their principle of life is interior, their tendency toward the good self-willed. Precepts, which, by binding men, bring about the state of slavery connected with a morality of the commandments, are *exterior* forces. But Christians possess *within* themselves their moral principle of judgment and of virtue. The written law has been abolished: they are moved and inspired by the Holy Spirit who lives in them. In other words, the Holy Spirit gives simultaneously life and the law of this life, the source of fullness and an interior direction toward it, as well as reasons for making specific choices in particular cases. Indeed, He infuses in us the life of God, grace, which has its own power. This power can well be called a law, since it is both strength and principle of action, and its directives are both definite and obligatory. We are led to think as God thinks and to act as He acts, that is, out of love. The life and law of the Spirit is the "law of charity" (Gal. 5:14). Charity is life, because it springs up from within the soul. It does not command; it attracts and quickens. St. Augustine comments very exactly: *"Dilige et quod vis fac!"*—"Love and do what you will!"

Such is the liberty St. Paul preached to all his converts: "All things are permissible to me" (1 Cor. 6:12, 10:23; Col. 2:16); "Why should my liberty be condemned?" (1 Cor. 10:29; Gal. 2:4). It was inevitable that souls who were insufficiently spiritual would abuse such an unqualified and boldly affirmed liberation. These turned their liberty to license, and St. Paul was obliged to remind them that a religious emancipation does not authorize the violation of rights or morality: "Yes, brothers, you have been called to liberty; only do not use liberty as an occasion for sensuality, but in love serve one another" (Gal. 5:13). Because they are slaves of Christ, Christians are completely independent of men and of sin (Rom. 6: 18, 22). On the other hand, the demands of charity control each man's exercise of liberty: "Independent though I am of all men, I make myself everybody's slave to win the more converts" (1 Cor. 9:19). "All things are permissible, but not all things are helpful. All things are permissible, but not all things build up character. Everyone should seek his neighbor's advantage rather than his own" (1 Cor. 10:23 *et sq.*)

In reality, Christian morality, which is a morality of the Holy Spirit and a morality of sonship, is essentially a morality of charity: "Let everything you do be regulated

by love" (1 Cor. 16:14). And "God's love is poured
forth in our hearts by the Holy Spirit who has been given
us" (Rom. 5:5). For this reason, its proper designation is
"the charity of the Spirit" (Rom. 15:30). Charity is constantly being related to the Holy Spirit[21] as a fruit to its
root (Gal. 5:22) or an effect to its cause (Col. 1:8). We
may speak equivalently of walking in the Spirit or of
walking in charity (Rom. 8:4 and Eph. 5:2); of being
sanctified by the Spirit or by charity, Rom. 15:16 and
Eph. 1:4); of one or the other as the force which establishes the body of Christ (Eph. 2:22 and 4:16; 1 Cor.
8:1). In a word, charity is the plenitude of this unique
and sovereign Law which is that of the Spirit (Rom. 8:2,
13:10).

Charity is not only the most excellent way to perfection (1 Cor. 12:31), but it is perfection itself, giving
value and consistency to all the other virtues, which it
unites, as it were, into a solid cluster (Col. 3:14). Too
much insistence has been placed on faith as the unique
principle of Pauline morality; for if it is true that the
"just man lives by faith," it is insofar as faith obtains from
God a sort of resurrection from the dead, that is, grace
and the purification from sin. But, in the moral life, this
faith is inconceivable without love;[22] it "expresses itself in
love" (Gal. 5:6). Further, without love, the greatest gifts
and the most beautiful virtues are without value: "If I

should speak the languages of men and of angels but have no love I am no more than a noisy gong and a clanging cymbal. . . . I am nothing. . . . It profits me nothing" (1 Cor. 13:1–3).

This love is first of all the love God has for us in Christ (Rom. 8:39). Transmitted by the Holy Spirit, it becomes our own and makes us capable of the same kind of love as God Himself. Consequently, the Holy Spirit, having engendered the baptized to divine life, enables them to love their heavenly Father with a love which, if it is not equal to His, is at least of the same nature. They are, as it were, on the same level with Him and can truly live in his company (Eph. 1:4). Christians are those who love God (1 Cor 2:9; Rom. 8:28) with a love of gratitude and of religious praise. Just as profession of faith is impossible without the illumination of the Holy Spirit— "no one can say 'Jesus is the Lord,' except under the influence of the Holy Spirit" (1 Cor. 12:3)—and just as hope is made to abound by the Holy Spirit (Rom. 15:13), so too it is the Holy Spirit who, in revealing to the children of God the treasures of love in the heart of their Father, makes them love as God loves: "What God holds ready for those who love him, he has revealed to us through his Spirit, who fathoms all things, even the depths of God. Who among men knows the inner thoughts of a man save the man's spirit within him? Even so, the thoughts of God no one knows but the Spirit of God. Now we have not received the spirit of the world, but the Spirit imparted by God. *Thus we are able to recognize the gifts bestowed on us by God*" (1 Cor. 2: 11–13).

The gift which summarizes all others is that of the well-beloved Son: "He has not spared even his own Son but has delivered him for us all" (Rom. 8:32). The Holy Spirit reveals to the faithful the infinity of love implied by the agony of the Cross and, as it were, immobilized on Calvary. The Lord had announced to His apostles that the Holy Spirit would teach them to understand (Jn. 14:16, 15:26, 16:13–14). Under His light Christians perceive the divine charity in the passion of Jesus. Nothing will be able to separate them from it (Rom. 8:39). "Love for Christ [crucified] impels us" (2 Cor. 5:14). This means that the love of Christ sacrificing Himself for us engenders our love for Him. Under the light of the Holy Spirit we understand the gratuitousness of His love and draw from it the practical consequences for our own lives: "Love for Christ impels us. We have come to the conclusion that since one died for all, therefore all died, and that Christ died for all, in order that they who are alive may no longer live for themselves, but for him who died for them and rose again. (2 Cor. 5:14–16).

Charity is more than an ascendancy; it is also a pressure and an impelling force. Born of the contemplation of the crucified Christ, it permeates our soul and determines all its acts. It preserves our soul in the permanent (Eph. 6:24) and personal possession of its Lord whom it is "impelled" to serve. We give our life to Christ as He gave His for us: "I live by faith in the Son of God, who loved me and sacrificed himself for me" (Gal. 2:20).

Because the charity infused by the Holy Spirit is that of God Himself and of Christ, the sons of God, who live in Christ, are brought to love their brothers as the Father and the Son love them. It is a law of nature: "Therefore, follow God's example, as his very dear children, and let your conduct be guided by love, as Christ also loved us and delivered himself for us as an offering to God, a sacrifice that has an agreeable fragrance" (Eph. 5:1–2). Charity is the trait that most typifies the resemblance between the sons and their Father in heaven. The example of Christ makes it clear that this love must extend to the point of total gift, of consecration: "In charity make yourselves the religious slaves of one another" (Gal. 5:13), exactly as you would of the Lord himself (Matt. 6:24). This love is a debt of which we can never acquit ourselves entirely (Rom. 13:8), for it is the only manner we have of proving to God our gratitude for His gifts. In an act of service to our neighbor, we both love and help our brother, and love God, offering to Him a spiritual sacrifice of thanksgiving.

There are then not two virtues of charity, but only one, the two objects of which cannot be dissociated. This is clearly seen in such forceful expressions as:

> Let there be no unpaid debt except the debt of mutual love, because he who loves his neighbor has fulfilled the Law. For the commandments: "You shall not commit adultery; you shall not kill; you shall not steal; you shall not covet"; and if there is any other commandment, are all summed up in this saying, "You shall love your neighbor as yourself." Love does no evil to a neighbor. Love therefore is the complete fulfillment of the Law (Rom. 13:8–10). In love serve one another. Why, the whole Law is fulfilled by the observance of the one precept, "You shall love your neighbor as yourself" (Gal. 5:13–14). Help bear one another's burdens, and so you will fulfill the law of Christ (Gal. 6:2). We are clothed with love (Col. 3:14), exactly as we are clothed with Christ himself (Gal. 3:27).

Charity, which unites the individual to Christ, will also be the binding force within the Christian community. The Holy Spirit strengthens this community (Eph. 4:2–4; Phil. 2:1) and leads its members to be "of one charity, one soul, one thought" (Phil. 2:2). Their fraternal charity will be colored by tenderness (Rom. 12:10; 1 Thess. 4:9); it will teach them the secret of forgetting themselves (Rom. 15:1), to seek the good and the joy of their neighbor (1 Cor. 13:5, 10:24, 33); it will enable them to encourage the fainthearted and support the weak (1 Thess. 5:14; 1 Cor. 8:9–10, 9:22), whose infirmities they themselves will bear (Rom. 15:1). It will always aim at peace, seeking to harmonize their own reactions with those of brothers the farthest removed from them in taste and thought (Rom. 12:16). In this way, fraternal charity "edifies" (Rom. 14:1; 1 Cor. 8:1 *et sq.*) the entire Church as well as each individual soul.

Such an adaptation on the part of the Christian to the most minute and changeable circumstances of daily life requires sharpness of judgment and at the same time a keen moral instinct. The legalism of contemporary Jewish morality had attempted to foresee the maximum number of possible "cases" that the just man would encounter and to dictate his reactions. The final result was a hedge of precepts and interdictions so thick that it smothered the soul and, at best, could be known only by an intellectual elite, who had become a group of veritable casuists. St. Paul's great innovation in the history of morality was to announce the abolition of the Law. He knew by the prophet Jeremias that at the coming of the Messias, God would replace the juridical covenant, engraved on tablets of stone, with a law, engraved on the hearts of His elect, a law that would enable them to know His exact will (Heb. 8:10–11). He substitutes, therefore, for the rigid and exterior obligations of the letter, the interior inspiration of the Holy Spirit (2 Cor.

3:3). The Holy Spirit transmits His light to the conscience (Rom. 8:16, 9:1), which henceforth rules each moral life in particular, whatever its circumstances— wealth or poverty, prosperity or adversity (Phil. 4:11). In conscience the Christian possesses a faculty that makes him aware of God's will for him and enables him to conform intelligently to it in all circumstances. It makes inquiries about the moral value of a particular act and its relationship to the demands of faith (1 Cor. 10:25, 27). Without recourse to an exterior authority, and without letting itself be swayed by the conduct of others, it judges and commands what must be done or avoided. Whereas a morality of the Commandments presupposes subjects that are minors who obey blindly (Gal. 4:1–5), the morality of liberty and of love can be lived only by mature persons, by adults, whose age in Christ is measured by the maturity of their moral judgment (1 Cor. 14:20; Eph. 4:13–14). In other words, the Christian, freed from the slavery of the Law, is an *autonomous* person; he makes his own choices. Conscience assures him real freedom in harmonizing his religious beliefs and his daily living.

No longer an exact obedience to a general rule, prescribed once and for all, virtue is now determined by the rightness of our intentions and the nature of our motives (Acts 23:1; 2 Cor. 4:2; 2 Tim. 1:3). It is not fear of punishment that prompts us to act, but rather the demands of conscience (Rom. 13:5); in other words, we act freely, by choice, and out of love for the good. According to what God Himself suggests at this particular moment, in concrete terms, conscience judges whether this particular word or this particular action corresponds to what God wishes. It is defiled if we act contrary to this light (Tit. 1:15; Heb. 9:14, 10:2, 22); it remains spotless and pure if we are faithful to this light. Thus, conscience is the seat of moral responsibility: "Assuredly we are confident that we have a good conscience, and are resolved to act uprightly in every respect" (Heb. 13:18; cf. 2 Cor. 1:12; Acts 24:16). We are never authorized to act without having consulted this immanent judge of our least thoughts and of the slightest movements of our heart. If we act blindly and by chance, even though conforming materially to the common rule, we sin (Rom. 14:23).

Conscience, united to knowledge of God and to faith (1 Cor. 8:7, 10; 1 Tim. 1:19, 3:9; 2 Tim. 1:3), is clearly the immediate rule of our moral life; it seeks opportunities for action; it decides what is useful or beneficial to our neighbor (1 Cor. 6:12, 10:23), what is likely to edify him or scandalize him. It is quite remarkable that the word "conscience" is used in the New Testament for the first time in a text relative to fraternal charity, which develops the principles of the new morality (1 Cor. 8:7–12; cf. 1 Tim. 1:5). According to this text, many Corinthians knew that Christians were permitted to eat meat offered in idol worship, since the gods of paganism were a pure creation of the mind. But certain converts, although they shared the same speculative conviction, were reluctant to eat this food. Not yet rid of their former attitude toward idols, they still regarded the eating of food that had been offered in the temples as a participation in idol worship. St. Paul praises the knowledge of the first group, but makes it clear that their certitude, correct though it be, does not give them the right to act. They must also take into account their weak brothers, who could be scandalized by their conduct. Thus, the two great complementary principles of Christian morality are: on the one hand, faith which reveals to us what in itself is most pleasing to God; on the other, fraternal charity, which here and now puts forth the good of one's neighbor. The Holy Spirit and conscience suggest exactly what must be done. St. Paul does not hesitate to write: "If food—the most indifferent of things—leads to my brother's sinning, never will I eat meat" (1 Cor. 8:13). In the final analysis, it is the love of one's neighbor that makes conscience and Christian morality explicit.

The preceding example shows that St. Paul, who was the freest of Christians and the most docile to the Holy Spirit, nevertheless took into account factors such as prejudices, heredity, and the weakness of others, as well as the customs and traditions of the Church,[23] the latter, notably when it was a question of the liturgy or of the attitude of men and women in congregational worship.

He reminds us forcefully that "what everyone else is doing" cannot be despised. It is impossible to live in society without being faithful to certain usages, concerned about good order and about that propriety which is a matter of self-respect as much as of fraternal charity:

> Take thought for decent conduct in the sight of all men (Rom. 12:17). I exhort you, brothers, to watch those who cause dissensions and scandals contrary to the doctrine you have learned; avoid them (Rom. 16:17). Conduct yourselves as children of light. The effects of light are every kind of goodness and justice and truth (Eph. 5:9). In conclusion, brothers, whatever is true, whatever is honorable, whatever just, whatever pure, whatever lovable, whatever merits praise—if there be any virtue, if anything worthy of praise—such are the things you should keep in mind (Phil. 4:8).

It goes without saying that St. Paul presupposes the demands of the natural law and of common sense: "Does not nature itself teach you . . ." (1 Cor. 11:14). In violating the order of nature, you do "what is not fitting."[24] Although he was a mystic, endowed with more gifts of the Spirit than all the Corinthians put together, and proud of it besides (1 Cor. 14:18), St. Paul demands that his disciples exercise sound judgment (1 Cor. 14:20; Tit. 2:5–6) and respect the basic orientation of all nature to God in regulating such things as the proper use of sexual relations (1 Cor. 5:1, 6:13, 18, 7:3–9), good con-

duct (Tit. 2:3), food (1 Cor. 9:4; 1 Tim. 4:4—"Everything that has been created by God is good, and nothing
is to be rejected that is received with thanksgiving." Cf.
Col. 3:21–23; Tit. 1:15: "To the clean, all things are
clean."), family life (1 Tim. 5:8, 14), respect for parents
(Eph. 6:1) and the aged (1 Tim. 5:1), obedience to law-
fully constituted authority (Rom. 13:1–7), which is
neither servility nor obsequiousness, and the right to a
salary (1 Cor. 9:7), a correlative of the right to work—the
lazy man has no right to eat. On this point, St. Paul con-
tinues the Israelite tradition that made laziness the most
ignoble of vices (Sir. 22:1–2); his lengthy and solemn
condemnation of idleness makes one think that he would
not have been very favorably inclined to excessive leisure:

> We command you, brothers, by the authority of our
> Lord Jesus Christ, to hold yourselves aloof from brothers
> leading idle lives, not in keeping with the instructions
> they received from us. You yourselves certainly know
> how you are in duty bound to follow our example. We
> did not lead an idle life among you, neither did we
> eat anybody's food free of charge. On the contrary we
> worked day and night in fatiguing labor and struggle to
> avoid being a burden to any of you. It is not that we
> have not the right. Our purpose was to give you a model
> in our conduct for your imitation. Even when we were
> with you, we gave you the command: If anyone is unwill-

ing to work, do not let him eat. And now we hear that some among you live in idleness and do no work, but meddle in the work of others. Such persons we command and exhort by the authority of the Lord Jesus Christ quietly to earn their own living. . . . If anyone refuses to obey the directions we give in this letter, note him and do not associate with him. Thus he will be put to shame (2 Thess. 3:6–14).

These many admonitions should not make us think that St. Paul was forced to return to a morality of the Commandments and to make virtue synonymous with propriety. Nothing could be farther from the truth. It is the spirit in which all things are done that matters, e.g., the spirit in which Christians take their place at table, "in faith and charity" (Rom. 14:2, 15), cherish their wives (Eph. 5:25), pay their taxes (Rom. 13:6–7), etc. Christians are under the direction of the Holy Spirit, who is life and youth,[25] and whose action is marked always by regeneration and renewal (Tit. 3:5). Where the Holy Spirit operates, everything is rejuvenated and transformed;[26] the most ordinary situations in life and the most humble actions become completely different in the way they are motivated and carried out. We live "in Christ" and are transformed into His image: "We render service which is new and according to the Spirit, not old and according to the letter" (Rom. 7:6). "Do not conform to this world's way of life, but be transformed by the renewal of your mind, that you may investigate the will of God—all that is good, all that is acceptable to him, all that is perfect" (Rom. 12:2).

This "manifestation" of the Holy Spirit (1 Cor. 12:7) in Christians is a work of *light*. The Spirit of wisdom and of revelation "illumines the eyes of the heart" (Eph. 1: 17–18; Heb. 6:4), in order to make God more perfectly known (Heb. 8:10–11) and to show forth the immensity of His gifts (1 Cor. 2:11–12), especially the inexpressible love that Christ has for us. It is only the interior man, strengthened and enlightened by the Holy Spirit, who has the power "to grasp fully, together with all the saints, what is the breadth and length and height and depth (of this mystery), and to know Christ's love which surpasses knowing, in order to be perfected and to bring to realization God's fullness" (Eph. 3:18–19). Christians receive an increase of power as regards love, which permits them to understand more exactly the four dimensions of the charity Christ bears us, in other words, its fullness, its immensity. More specifically, the Holy Spirit makes souls who love understand that the charity of Christ is immeasurable, without limit, inexpressible. Henceforth we are capable of knowing . . . the unknowable! Christians thus arrive at a negative knowledge, that of the "in-finite"; they realize that the intensity and depth of this love exceed all human measure and are beyond their comprehension: "No one," comments St. Thomas, "can know how much Christ loves us!"

The Holy Spirit intervenes in such a special way in the relationship between the sons of God and their Father that He is defined as the bond of union between God and us (2 Cor. 13:13; cf. Phil. 2:1). He incites and directs our prayer:

> The Spirit comes to aid our weakness. For we do not know what we should pray for as we ought, but the Spirit himself pleads for us with unutterable sighs. And he who searches hearts knows what the Spirit desires and that he, in accord with God's designs, pleads for the saints (Rom. 8:26–27).

Each time that a true prayer of praise, supplication, or thanksgiving rises toward God, it is always the Spirit who gives it the form needed for it to be received (1 Cor. 14:14–19; Eph. 5:18–20): "Pray always by the Spirit, using every kind of entreaty and petition" (Eph. 6:18). There is no better way to say that the Christian life is first of all a religious life, and that, being completely "spiritual," it flourishes in contemplation.

Christians, led and enlightened in this way by the Holy Spirit, have their outlook renewed (Eph. 4:23); they learn to judge everything in a Christian way (1 Cor. 7:40). What a serious thing it would be to extinguish this living flame by hindering its manifestations or by refusing to understand: "Do not extinguish the Spirit" (1 Thess. 5:19). A person who is mentally ill cannot use his intelligence and liberty, because these faculties are, as it were, chained. In the same way, although each baptized person is adopted by God, incorporated into Christ, and receives the Holy Spirit, a certain number, impervious to every impulse of the Spirit, are deprived of a true "spiritual sense." They may be virtuous, in the Jewish or pagan sense, they may obey the Law and live morally correct lives, but they lack supernatural intelligence and they live always as children. It is all a question of *pneuma!*

The Holy Spirit is our source of *power* as well as our guide.[27] When we say that He equips us with all the virtues (Phil. 1:19), we mean that He fills us with strength. He is generosity itself, and, like all perfect energies, His assistance combines power and gentleness. He consoles at the same time as He encourages and strengthens. "The assistance of the Holy Spirit" to which the Church's first historian attributes her increase (Acts 9:31) is made up of light, strength, encouragement, consolation, peace, and joy. According to Philippians 2:1–2, this constant support is also marked by tenderness; and so the role of the Holy Spirit is often spoken of as a maternal role. There will always be in the Church men who are especially endowed, masters of the *paraclesis* (Rom. 12:8; 1 Cor. 14:3; 1 Tim 4:13), who have a gift for consoling and comforting hearts (Eph. 6:22; Col. 2:2, 4:8), particularly those worn out by effort or assailed by trials (1 Thess. 3:7; 2 Cor. 7:4, 6, 13); it is the God of all mercy who through them transmits His gentle and beneficial help, like a physician dressing a wound. But every Christian who assists his brother and offers him support is also the instrument of the Holy Spirit, especially when it is a question of rehabilitating sinners (1 Thess. 4:8; 2 Cor. 2:7).

Having drunk of the Holy Spirit since the day of their baptism (1 Cor. 12:13), and having been marked with His seal for the day of final redemption, Christians will not only avoid all that can grieve this Spirit of holiness (Eph. 4:30; cf. 1 Thess. 4:8), but they will seek to "breathe in the spirit" (Ps. 119:31), to be more and more filled with the Spirit, as with a full-bodied wine, which, taken in abundance, makes one think, speak, and act in a way other than ordinary.

> Do not get drunk on wine, which is a cause of debauchery, but fill yourselves with the Spirit (Eph. 5:17). Cf. Acts 2:4–18: They were all filled with the Holy Spirit and began to speak in other tongues, as the Holy Spirit prompted them to give utterance. . . . Others said in mockery, "They are full of sweet wine." But Peter, presenting himself with the Eleven, raised his voice and addressed them. . . . "These men are not drunk, as you suppose, since it is only nine o'clock in the morning. But

this is what was foretold by the prophet Joel: 'It shall happen in the last days, says God, that I will pour forth my Spirit on all mankind.'" (Prophets seized by the Spirit of God were traditionally likened to men overcome by wine [cf. Jer. 23:9]; souls flooded with grace are in a *sobria ebrietas*, etc.).

"Filled with the Holy Spirit," Christians see all things in a different way; they are capable of accomplishing wonders, for they are moved from on high. As a consequence, they will advance from stage to stage of the moral life according as they are more or less docile to the Holy Spirit (Gal. 3:2–6). From first justification to final plenitude their progress knows no fixed limits, for it is that of God's life (Eph. 3:19) received in increasing abundance:

> Not that I have already attained this ideal, or have already been made perfect, but I press on, hoping that I may lay hold of it, since Christ has laid hold of me. Brothers, I do not consider that I have reached it. But one thing I do: forgetting what is past, I strain toward what is ahead. With my eyes fixed on the goal, I press on to the prize in store for those who have received from above God's call in Jesus Christ. All of us, then, who have reached maturity must agree, and if in any point you disagree, in this God will enlighten you. Meanwhile, whatever the point we have reached, let us continue to advance in orderly fashion (Phil. 3:12–16).

Having been purified from sin and made holy, beginners are in *Christo*, it is true, but like children, and even like babes, they remain in many ways "carnal" and very human (1 Cor. 2:14—3:4). As they grow up and draw nearer to perfection, they become more spiritual. Full-grown men in Christ (Eph. 4:13–15) who have attained their adult stature are "spiritual" men (Gal. 6:1). The true Christian lives entirely by the breath of the Holy Spirit. According to Pauline ethics, "spiritual" is a synonym of "perfect." Once again, we see how morality according to the Spirit is a morality of sonship. We are not true children of God until we are sufficiently spiritualized to enter into intimate relations with the Father in heaven, who is pure spirit.

Pauline morality has an easily discernible Trinitarian structure. The Father, having taken the initative in salvation out of love, communicates His grace and life to His children. It is He who makes us pass from "nothingness into existence" (Rom. 4:17), "who gives life to all things" (1 Tim. 6:13), and "who even raises us from the dead" (Heb. 11:19). This gift of the Father requires from Christians total self-oblation and a corresponding response of gratitude, which they will manifest particularly by their fidelity; it requires also that they use the gifts they have received according to the intention of the God who gave them; in other words, for His glory.

Now the will of the Father—the Christian vocation—is that the faithful be true images of the crucified and glorious Christ. The moral life consists then in perfecting this resemblance to the Lord, in being inspired with His thoughts and sentiments, in imitating His virtues, in living in a symbiosis with Him, until the day when they will rejoin Him in heaven to reign with Him forever.

Because such an assimilation is impossible for a man left to his own strength, the third person of the Holy Trinity takes over the Christian at the time of his baptism; He enlightens him, guides him, entreats him, and strengthens him in every way. We have only to let ourselves be renewed and rejuvenated interiorly from day to day. Under the movement of the Holy Spirit, the moral life is a spiritual life in the strictest sense; for the sons of God become divine only when they become spiritual: "May the grace of the Lord Jesus Christ, and the love of God, and the communion of the Holy Spirit be with you all" (2 Cor. 13:13; cf. 2 Cor. 1:21–22).

To live by faith means to participate in this life of the Trinity; it means to believe with one's whole being that the three divine Persons do in reality communicate their life to us.

CHAPTER 5
The Beauty of the Moral Life

ST. BEDE COLLEGE
PERU, ILL.
LIBRARY

THE FRUITS OF THIS DIVINE EDUCATION CAN BE NOTHING other than magnificently rich. When, in the evening of his life, St. Paul reflected upon Christian morality, whose main axes he had determined, he found it radiant with beauty. For him, to obey truth, to do good, to live in beauty were one and the same thing. "Those who have faith in God must be anxious to excel in beautiful works" (Tit. 3:8).

This conception of moral beauty is rich in meaning; it contains the qualities of nobility, integrity, and glory, of perfection and completion; it is opposed to ugliness which is a characteristic of vice; finally it implies excellence—the beautiful is the perfect good, uniting order, measure, and harmony. It is not only appealing and attractive, but it is preferred before all else, and it is praiseworthy because it is good.

This spiritual beauty that St. Paul asks of his disciples is the radiant splendor of grace, received from God and revealing itself in the most varied ways in concrete daily circumstances: "Christ redeemed us to have a people zealous for beautiful works" (Tit. 2:14). He wished his Church to be "resplendent, devoid of blemish or wrinkle or anything of the kind, but holy and flawless" (Eph. 5:27). The harmony between the exterior conduct and the interior grace of Christians gives an esthetic quality to their morality; it has measure, order, balance, decency, and religious gravity. All the virtues adorn and embellish the regenerated soul that draws life from God dwelling within it. As it is characteristic of beautiful deeds to be manifest (1 Tim. 5:25), this splendor of virtue becomes a sign and an ornament of the true Faith.

Pastors must furnish the model of virtue (Tit. 2:7), but so also must women (Tit. 2:10), especially widows (Tit. 5:10), and those who are rich (I Tim. 6:18), for these have special opportunities to manifest their love and thus to radiate the charity of God himself. All that is excellent, made with proportion and style, radiating good and attracting it, merits the epithet beautiful; and every act of a truly spiritual life ought to be so named. At the time of his baptism, Timothy made a *magnificent* profession of faith before a multitude of witnesses (1 Tim. 6:12), after the example of Christ who *heroically* bore witness to the truth before Pilate (1 Tim. 6:13). St. Paul fought victoriously the *noble* fight of the faith (2 Tim. 4:7), keeping it intact in spite of attacks or the dangers of depredation. Each Christian must take his share of suffering, like a soldier worthy of the name, *courageous* (2 Tim. 2:3), serving his Lord with *pride* and fidelity (1 Tim. 1:18). To live in beauty in the Church of God means to keep one's promises, consequently to have a sense of honor (cf. 2 Cor. 8:21), and, by this fundamental integrity to receive the approval of God and of men (1 Tim. 3:7). Whereas the conscience of sinners is defiled, a good conscience is pure and beautiful (Heb. 10:22, 13:

18). A true son of God must necessarily reflect his noble race. Reproducing the morality of his Father, he is an "epiphany" of the divine beauty.

In counseling his disciples: "Wish to appear beautiful before God," Epictetus was only repeating the Platonic ideal, which identified the idea of the beautiful with the divinity. According to this ideal, the secret of true virtue and happiness is to contemplate Beauty, to live by it, and to conform oneself to it. Adapting himself to the psychology of his contemporaries, St. Paul emphasizes the splendor of the new religion. The Epistles to Timothy and to Titus consider the visible Church as a city built on a mountaintop, which cannot escape notice (Matt. 5: 14). She commands the attention of the pagan world; each one of her members is a shining example of virtue; her hierarchy is of high caliber and noteworthy. Old men as well as women and slaves have a distinctive character; young people are prudent (Tit. 2:6); all manifest a becoming dignity. The religious gravity in question here is that which belongs to holy persons, who have become the temples of God. Thus, a corollary of religious consecration is dignity of life (1 Tim. 2:2), which results in the *decorum* characteristic of all who profess to serve God (1 Tim. 2:9–10). And so, each Christian possesses and reflects this saving grace received from Christ, which is so attractive to unbelievers living in darkness. It must not be forgotten that the first meaning of the Greek word for "grace" is beauty; grace, therefore, signifies not only what is gratuitous, but what is gracious.

This is corroborated by the commentaries of the Fathers of the Church: "God has not only delivered us from sin. He has made us beautiful, lovable, and attractive" (St. John Chrysostom on Eph. 1:6).

> We are new, or rather we were new, for now we have grown old and are near death. Nevertheless, if we wish, we can repair this shameful decrepitude. We can no longer do it by baptism, but we can do it by penance. If we have some symptom of old age, let us cast it away. If already we bear some wrinkles, spots, or blemishes, let us remove them and recover our pristine beauty, in order that the King may love us in this renewed beauty. Although we have perhaps fallen into a state of extreme ugliness, we can once again find the charm and grace of which David speaks: "Listen, my daughter, and see; incline thine ear; forget thy people and the house of thy father, and the King will greatly desire thy beauty" (*Idem.* on Heb. 8:13).

"It is not only the word of the saints, it is their very countenances which shine with a spiritual grace" (Hom. III, *To the People of Antioch*). According to St. Gregory of Nyssa, St. Paul prayed for the Ephesians, "so that they might preserve in its integrity, for the coming of the Lord, beauty of body, soul, and mind" (*Creation of Man* 8, PG XLIV, 145). And St. Athanasius says that when

Divine Wisdom made men divine, He made them beautiful:

> So that the things made might not only exist, but might exist in beauty, it pleased God to have his Wisdom condescend to creatures. A figure and a trace of his image was placed in all creatures together and in each one in particular, in order that the things made might be filled with wisdom, and that the works of God might appear worthy of him. For just as our own word is the image of the true word of God, so too the wisdom which comes into us is the image of his true Wisdom, an image by which we have the power so to know and think, that we are capable of receiving the creative wisdom and, through it, of knowing the Father" (II *Discourse against the Arians*, 78; PG XXVI, 312).

"We do not believe in Christ in order to become good men, but in order to become perfect men, both beautiful and good" (Clement of Alexandria, *Strom.* VI, 17; 149–150). St. Augustine concludes all the prescriptions of his *Rule* by this wish: "The Lord grant that you may observe all these things as becomes lovers of spiritual beauty" (PL XXXII, 1384).

It is incumbent upon all Christians, as sons of light, to make the "beautiful and saving grace" communicated to them by Christ resplendent by the dignity of their lives (Tit. 2:11). To live in beauty is thus not only a moral requirement but an entire spirituality. St. Paul directed the Cretan slaves to "be submissive to their masters, to please them in every respect, not to oppose them, not to pilfer, but to show utter and heartfelt fidelity, *for thus in all their actions they will reflect credit on the doctrine of God our Savior*" (Tit. 2:9–10). This doctrine is the revelation that God has made of Himself in His Son, in order that all men may know and love Him. But, we may ask, how can men add anything to the beauty of this religion, how can they "adorn" it? The complement of beauty required of them is good works that day by day complete the "edification"* of the Church, which is the house of God and the column of truth. One does not decorate an ugly object with a beautiful ornament; this would only accentuate its ugliness. An ornament belongs with an object worthy of being enhanced by it and fit to receive it; the ornament thus becomes a form of homage, a tribute paid to beauty. The object adorned is thereby made more noticeable and more appealing; just as, for example, a painting is more easily noticed and admired if it is in a beautiful frame; a king, if he is in royal robes. The adornment is therefore a sign of merit and of value.

In adorning Christian doctrine with their virtues, Christians draw attention to it, making it more attractive by emphasizing the respect it deserves. By the simple fact

---

* Translator's note: the French word *édification*, like the Latin, has the double significance of "building up" and "edifying."

that they live religiously, they not only give a testimony of honor to God's revelation, but a permanent sermon, which incites the admiration and often the envy of "those outside." One can even say that Christian doctrine truly becomes more beautiful by thus giving proof of its efficacy. A teaching that no one admires is a poor thing. It may be true in itself, but it is as useless as a book in the hands of an illiterate man, as worthless as a treasure at the bottom of the sea. When Christians, on the other hand, live their faith and put into act the suggestions of the Holy Spirit, they adorn and enhance the doctrine of Christ by beautiful works, showing forth its saving, beneficent, and consoling character. Thus any man who adapts his conduct to the prescriptions of the Gospel can augment its "virtue" of conversion and increase its beauty!

It is understandable that the aristocracy of the Empire who embraced the Christian faith—the senators, magistrates, and officers—could adorn the new doctrine with their prestige and bring about its growth; their submission paid homage to its truth, proclaimed its merits, and increased its power of attraction. But slaves? How could they, the most abject and obscure of men, aspire to this work of splendor? Their tastes were so low; their moral judgment so depraved! For a religion to be adopted by the dregs of the population was not a recommendation; rather, it discredited the Gospel. This was the objection made by Celsus and by other distinguished men of the imperial epoch: Christianity received its followers from among the inferior classes of society, and from women, children, and slaves!

But the assertion of St. Paul is well-grounded. If the fact that a great number of slaves accepted the faith was not of itself a recommendation of the Gospel, their Christian life became the best of all recommendations. The worst sinner, once he is converted, can become a saint; and it is this transformation that fills men with wonder. All the good these humble souls henceforth did they owed to their new religion, which made them obedient, reserved, honorable, respectful, and dignified. Their masters who were the least favorable to Christianity had their attention drawn to it because of the unmistakable moral transformations it wrought. Christian slaves were in reality the best example of the saving cure from sin, which was accomplished in and by the Church.

And so, those whom the pagan world most often despised were chosen to "adorn" the truth of the Gospel. By their virtues they were able to convert entire families. Irascible masters noticed that their slaves were never angry; cruel masters remarked the gentleness and respect of their servants; those deceitful in business observed that their slaves were scrupulously honest; the sensual were amazed that their converted slaves remained sober and chaste; the fastidious and delicate discovered in their slaves examples of true gentlemen. Where did their slaves learn these principles of life? Who gave them the strength to practice them?

Such a beauty cannot but attract, and it is ageless. To-day, as in the days of St. Paul, the Christian, no matter how humble or how obscure, is the child of God; he exists in Christ, and he possesses the strength of the Holy Spirit. It is inconceivable that the presence of Christ and the action of the Holy Spirit will not reveal themselves in some way, even to those least aware. Furthermore, the life of the Christian is a perpetual renewal and rejuvenation; ought he not then appear of another race than "those of the world"? He has a singular dignity: he is master of himself and he is free! He loves his neighbor, manifests benignity, compassion, and an untiring devotion toward all. He is filled always with serenity; even when he is tried, he is jubilant. The harmony of all his moral qualities makes him beautiful and attractive. Others are drawn by his peace, his optimism, his courage, and his happiness. He is gracious to everyone alike, and his sweetness and gentleness win him many hearts.

The moral life of Christians does indeed shine like a light in the darkness of the world, and its splendor convinces men of the truth of the faith. "Children of God, without blemish in the midst of a depraved and perverse generation, you shine, like heavenly luminaries in the world" (Phil. 2:15). To be glowing and radiant is the privilege of the spiritual, and it becomes a rule of life for the children of God.

> You have all been born to the light, to noonday brightness. We belong neither to night nor to darkness. And so we are not to sleep as do the rest of men, but to be vigilant and alert. Sleepers sleep at night and drunkards are drunk at night. But let us, who belong to the day, be alert. Let us put on the breastplate of faith and love, and for a helmet, the hope of salvation (1 Thess. 5:5–8). Let us lay aside the deeds prompted by darkness, and put on the armor of light. Let us conduct ourselves becomingly as in the day, not in revelry and drunkenness, not in debauchery and wantonness, not in strife and jealousy. But put on the Lord Jesus Christ (Rom. 13:12–14). Formerly you were darkness, now in the Lord you are light. Conduct yourselves as children of light. The effects of the light are every kind of goodness and justice and truth (Eph. 5:8–9).

"Whatever is manifest is light" (Eph. 5:13). It is God Himself who illumines the world in the person of His disciples. They are like vases of alabaster, diffusing a mellow brightness, transparent with the light they enclose; or like a multitude of torches scintillating in the deep night. No more than was John the Baptist, who was nevertheless so close to the Savior, the faithful are not themselves the source of light; they are only lamps. They "manifest" the radiating source of all brightness that they carry within them, and by the beauty of their moral lives they extend its effulgence. "The God who said, 'Let light shine from the midst of darkness' has shone in our hearts, to give enlightenment through the knowledge of God's glory, glowing in the face of Christ" (2 Cor. 4:6).

CHAPTER 6

"Pressing on Toward What Is Ahead"

THE CHRISTIAN LIFE IS A MAGNIFICENT THING. AND YET, for all its nobility, it does not have its fulfillment on earth. It is, in fact, so foreign to the conditions of this earthly life that it can be understood only in terms of its true home, heaven. We become Christians "to serve the living and true God, to await His Son from heaven" (1 Thess. 1:9), and, at the same time, "to live worthy of the God who calls [us] to his kingdom and glory" (1 Thess. 2:12; cf. 2 Thess. 1:5). We would be deceived, therefore, if death were the end of everything. Furthermore, the Christian life would be meaningless or it would be some other religion, because both faith and the moral life it inspires have their fulcrum, their very reason for being, in the fullness of the celestial life. A road has meaning only in terms of its destination.

> If it is merely for this life that we have placed our hope in Christ, we are the most pitiable of men. . . . If it is certain that the dead do not rise . . . why do we at every moment expose ourselves to danger? . . . If it was from human motives that I fought wild beasts at Ephesus, what use was it to me? If the dead are not raised, let us eat and drink since tomorrow we shall die (1 Cor. 15: 19, 29–32; cf. Gal. 3:4).

The link established between earth and heaven, between today and tomorrow, is so strong that our moral life, far from having any value in itself, takes its direction from this lofty perspective. What we must do is remain upright and blameless *until* the day of Christ (Phil. 1: 10). Our salvation, which has been begun, will be permanent only if we keep ourselves from evil and persevere in good; otherwise we will have believed in vain (1 Cor. 15: 2; 1 Tim. 2:5). St. Paul bases his own certitude of a completely happy life on the fact that he has preserved his faith in Christ to the end (2 Tim. 4:7).

The passage from earth to heaven will not be effected without an appearance before the tribunal of Christ the supreme Judge. Each conscience will be laid bare; its secret intentions disclosed; its actions judged:

> God will render to everyone according to his deeds: life eternal to those who by persevering in good deeds seek glory, honor, and immortality; wrath and indignation for rebellious spirits and for those who, refusing to submit to the truth, assent to iniquity (Rom. 2:6–8). We shall all stand before the judgment seat of God. . . . Everyone will render account of himself to God (Rom. 14:10–12; cf. Eph. 5:6). We must all be laid open to inspection before the tribunal of Christ, each to receive his due in keeping with the good or evil he has done while he was in the body (2 Cor. 5:10). Christ Jesus will come to judge the living and the dead (2 Tim. 4:1, 14).

The certitude of judgment and retribution cannot but weigh heavily in the decisions of every man who aspires to happiness. It fills the wicked with fear, sparks the courage of the indifferent, and strengthens the hope of the good. Christians live by faith and love, it is true, in the sense that divinely revealed truths and love of Christ are the basic motives of their choices and conduct; but they are also men, and the sanest kind of prudence requires that they take their own best interests into consideration. Our Lord Himself guaranteed that a total gift of self was an absolute assurance of beatitude: Blessed are the poor in spirit . . . ; Blessed are the meek. . . . In the same way, St. Paul stirs up the fervor of his disciples by re- minding them of the reward or punishment that awaits them. Not that he envisions life on earth merely as a time of preliminary proving at the end of which will be a final test—his conception of life is too lofty for that; but he applies a principle of justice, more specifically a law of nature, which requires us to do honor to the gift of God. To this end he uses metaphors of work, such as, "The laborer must earn his salary"; metaphors of sport: "The runner must train to win the prize"; of military life: "The soldier must fight to obtain victory"; and especially, of agriculture: "The tree must produce fruit; the harvest is in proportion to the sowing."

> Mark this: he who sows sparingly will also reap a scant harvest, and he who sows abundantly will also reap a bountiful harvest (2 Cor. 9:6). God is not mocked. A

man reaps just what he sows. He who sows in his corrupt
nature, from that corrupt nature reaps corruption. But
he who plants in the field of the spirit will reap life everlasting. In doing good let us not be discouraged, because
in due time we shall reap if we do not become careless
(Gal. 6:7–9; cf. Rom. 6:22–23; 8:13, 11:20–22; Phil. 1:
28; 3:18–21). Can it be that you are unaware that the
unjust will not inherit the kingdom of God? Make no
mistake; no fornicator, no idolator, no adulterer, no
pervert, no homosexual, no thief, no slave of avarice, no
drunkard, no addict of abusive language, no miser will
inherit the kingdom of God (1 Cor. 6:9–10; cf. Gal. 5:
21). On account of these sins the wrath of God comes
upon the unbelievers (Eph. 5:5–6.) A man will be re-
paid by the Lord for whatsoever good he does (Eph. 6:
8). As your reward you will receive the inheritance from
the Lord. . . . He who does a wrong will receive the
penalty for the wrong he did. There is no partiality (Col.
3:24–25). The rich who are liberal in sharing their goods
with others shall "provide for themselves a good foundation for the life to come, in order that they may lay hold
on the true life" (1 Tim. 6:19; cf. 2 Tim. 4:6). Work
out your salvation with fear and trembling (Phil. 2:12).

Some profess to be surprised that such a reiteration of
threats and promises is made to the "holy," who "exist in
Christ," believe in the unfailing love of God for them,
and are called to live in beauty.[28] Should they not act for
a higher motive? they ask. Are God's servants not charac-

terized by disinterestedness? They forget the two basic axes of revealed ethics. The first is theocentric: God is the Master; if He gives salvation gratuitously, He has a right to impose obedience, fidelity, and perseverance: demands which would amount to nothing if no sanctions were placed upon them. A God who is holy can call only those who are holy to live in His company; His immense generosity has as its corollary the stringency of His demands. The second axis of Pauline ethics is man's liberty and consequently his responsibility. For every gift there is a corresponding obligation. If man is truly master of his life and choices, he can orient them either toward good or toward evil; and since, on this earth, he remains "tempted" and must resist the solicitations of the flesh, it is actually an act of mercy on God's part to encourage his choices by the hope of reward and the fear of punishment. The Christian life is movement and growth: from infancy to maturity, from the beginning of the journey to its end, from the first foundation of the edifice to its completion, from the sowing to the harvest. How many occasions there are to deviate and to give way! The contributions of hope and of fear are not superfluous. To be surprised at this is to think of the Christian as a "hero," when in reality he is a sinner and a man constantly being saved.[29] Indeed, the two elements together constitute and define a Christian.

In any case, the present world is and will remain until

the end of time a place of suffering and death from which souls of any sensitivity at all cannot but hope to be delivered:

> Why, I count the sufferings of the present life as not worthy to be compared with the glory to come that will be revealed shining upon us. All creation awaits with eager longing the manifestations of the sons of God. For creation was made subject to vanity not by its own choice but by the will of him who made it subject, yet with the hope that creation itself would be delivered from its slavery to corruption, to enjoy the freedom that comes with the glory of the children of God. For we know that all creation groans and travails in pain until now. And not only that, but we ourselves who have the Holy Spirit as first fruits—we ourselves groan within ourselves, waiting for the adoption as sons, the redemption of our body. As yet, our salvation is only a matter of hope. Now there is no hope when the object which had been hoped for is seen. How can a man hope really for what he sees? But if we hope for what we do not see, we wait for it with patience (Rom. 8:19–25).

Faith gives great insight into the consummation of life in Christ. Christians know that "this short moment of our tribulation which weighs so lightly is producing for us an eternal weight of glory that is beyond all measure. And we direct our gaze not at what is seen but at what is unseen. For what we see is temporary, but what we do not see endures forever" (2 Cor. 4:17–18). The glory to come is the plenitude of the divine life which will be shared (1 Thess. 2:12; 2 Thess. 2:14; 2 Tim. 2:10), the crown of the victorious (1 Thess. 2:19; 2 Tim. 4:8–9) and of kings (Rom. 5:17; 1 Tim. 1:17), a beatitude which surpasses all expression and even imagination: "What no eye has ever seen, what no ear has ever heard, what no human heart has ever thought of, namely, the great blessings God holds ready for those who love Him, it is to us God has revealed them through his Spirit" (1 Cor. 2:9–10). A Christian worthy of the name, therefore, is essentially a man of hope who does not hesitate to affirm: "For me to die means gain" (Phil. 1:21; cf. Phil. 3:14).

If we remember that faith is not only belief in invisible realities, but the anticipated possession and guarantee of the blessings for which we hope (Heb. 11:1), then we will grasp the continuity from life on earth to life in heaven. They are but one life. It is absolutely impossible for the Christian, who is a son of God in the true sense, not to rejoin his Father. Grafted onto Christ and living in Christ here on earth, it is impossible for him not to contemplate Christ in glory. The Holy Spirit, who dwells in him, will gradually spiritualize him so that he can take his place in this divine home. A citizen of his heavenly fatherland, and enjoying its privileges even here on earth, the Christian will one day take up his abode definitively in this holy city (Phil. 3:20). In other words, it is not a question of just any happiness, or respite, or a reward accorded to virtue; it is not even a question of an abstract change from grace to glory; but rather, of living in the beloved and beatifying presence of the three divine Persons (1 Cor. 13:12; Eph. 1:4).

Whenever he attempts to explain the happiness that will be ours in heaven, St. Paul has recourse to his favorite expression—*to be, to live with Christ!*[30]—and this, for three reasons: divine predestination requires the elect to reproduce the image of the only-begotten and glorious Son in such a way that Christ will be surrounded in heaven by a multitude of brothers who, by their very presence, will give glory to His work of salvation (Rom. 8:29; cf. Eph. 1:10); grace, which is constantly being infused, unceasingly perfects this likeness here on earth—"God is faithful; it was he who called you into fellowship with his Son, Jesus Christ our Lord" (1 Cor. 1:9); and finally, Christ Himself died precisely in order that "we may have life in union with him" (1 Thess. 5:10). One person is with another when he is close to him and in his company; for example, when we say that we live with someone, we mean that we live in the same home with him. Thus, the formula "to be with Christ" expresses the double idea of proximity and community. It is true, of course, that even now the faithful are in Christ and live by His life. But "we know full well that while we are in the body we are exiled from the Lord, since we guide ourselves by faith, not by what is seen. We even have the courage to prefer to be exiled from the body and to be at home with the Lord" (2 Cor. 5:6–8).

The intense hope of being with Christ is the fruit of love, it is the hope of the faithful who are "constrained" by the charity of Christ, who have given themselves body and soul to their Lord, who aspire to see Him and to enjoy His presence. Since the "gathering together [of all the elect] with Christ" (2 Thess. 2:1) is a dogma of faith ("If we have died with him, we shall also live with him" [2 Tim. 2:11]), it is impossible for the Christian not to thrill with joy at the prospect of "being with the Lord forever" (1 Thess. 4:17); for where his treasure is, there is his heart. The same Apostle who confessed: "It is now no longer I who live, but Christ lives in me; and the life that I now live in this body, I live by faith in the Son of God, who loved me and sacrificed himself for me" (Gal. 2:20–21) feels himself growing impatient. "For me to live means Christ. . . . I desire to depart to be with Christ" (Phil. 1:21–23).

The moral life takes its direction from the certitude of this encounter. The neophyte of St. Paul's day was converted not only on the evidence of the resurrection of Christ (1 Cor. 15:1–2), but in the hope of the resurrection of all the dead (Acts 23:6, 26:5–7). If he dedicated his whole existence to the Lord, it was in the conviction that he would see Him and would live with Him eternally.

What value could "the goods of this world" have for him when, having set his mind on immortality and incorruptibility, he recognized the supreme advantage of knowing Christ (Phil. 3:8)? Possessed and, as it were, grasped by the omnipotence of Christ, he desired to seize Him fully in his turn (Phil 2:12–13) and to be more totally assimilated to Him. He imitated Christ as closely as possible by conformity to His thoughts and feelings. But he realized that the transformation would be perfect only in heaven; for, "to be with Christ" is not so much to see Him and to possess Him, as to have a share in *His glory, His* fidelity, *His* reign—to be one with Him!

This is to be taken in the most literal sense, because the Christian is called to resemble the glorious Christ even physically. From the time of baptism, when we are inserted as living members into the "spiritual body" of the Lord (1 Cor. 6:15, 12:27; Eph. 5:30), we participate in the efficacy of the resurrection of Christ (Col. 2:12). Our moral life consists in assimilating progressively the death and resurrection of Christ. This symbiosis of our inner man and Christ must necessarily have some repercussion on our bodies. The presence of Christ takes more and more hold on us, "marks" us (Gal. 6:17), and conforms us to His image. St. Paul writes that Christ "forms himself" in us (Gal. 4:19). By means of living in Christ, we live as Christ lives and we transform ourselves into Him. Since the eucharistic banquet is a "communion with the glorious body of Christ" which completes our incorporation in Him, our flesh, too, is affected by this vital contact. Furthermore, the Holy Spirit, who will complete the changing of our carnal bodies into spiritual bodies (1 Cor. 15:54), is preparing and anticipating their resurrection (2 Cor. 1:22, 5:5; Rom. 8:23). It is by means of His action in us now that the future resurrection will be possible, and that there will be a certain identity between our present body—though not in its fleshly aspect—and our glorified body: "If the Spirit of him who raised Jesus from the dead dwells in you, then he who raised Christ Jesus from the dead will also bring to life your mortal bodies because of the Spirit who dwells in you" (Rom. 8:11).

Finally, "just as we have borne the likeness of the man of dust, so shall we bear the likeness of the Heavenly One" (1 Cor. 15:49), the Lord of glory, who was the first to rise from the dead (Col. 1:18). Then our imitation of Christ will be complete. The Christian life will result in a most brilliant triumph: *"The Lord Jesus will refashion our lowly bodies, conforming them to his glorious body by an exercise of the power which enables him even to subject the universe to himself"* (Phil. 3:21). This is the completion of the new creation (2 Cor. 5:17–18).

This being true, the attitude of the Christian must be one of pressing on toward what is ahead (Phil. 3:13). Christians are defined as those who wait with love for the manifestation of the Lord.[31] In a sense, they count the days. Unless it is just an empty expression, we must understand the words of St. Paul as an indication of impatience: "Now our salvation is nearer than when we came to believe" (Rom. 13:11). We see the day approaching, the dawn is breaking (Heb. 10:25), the Lord is drawing near; He is coming; He is here. *Maranatha* (1 Cor. 16:22). There is no longer place for anxiety of any kind (Phil. 4:5–6). Since there remains only a little time to do good, we must accomplish it with courage and fervor (1 Cor. 7:29–31; Gal. 6:10). The Christian life is now completely enlightened, liberated, and made easy. We are so certain, and we are almost there (1 Cor. 1:9; 2 Tim. 2:11–13).

Joy and gladness are the climate of this existence in Christ (Phil. 3:1, 4:4), which is animated by the Holy Spirit (1 Thess. 16:6; Rom. 14:17; Gal. 5:22), and so we can speak very accurately of a "joy in the faith" (Phil. 1: 25) which is characteristic of the true Christian; he is always happy (2 Cor. 6:10). It is especially a question of joy in hope, however (Rom. 12:12, 15:13), a joy in the first fruits of eternal life. It burst forth spontaneously from those hearts that had been walled in by the desolation and despair of paganism and then suddenly saw light dawning. Hope was reborn, and their Christian joy was nothing other than this change from despair to hope. Anticipating the possession of the Beloved, it is one of the surest signs of a "participation in the marvelous powers of the world to come" (Heb. 6:4–5). Hope makes those who have relished its sweetness sing paeans of joy.

The happiness that comes from loving with true charity is permanent and unfailing.[32] *Agape*, which is the Greek word for charity, sounded for St. Paul's contemporaries a note of contentment, gladness, and joy.[33] In other words, among a thousand possible kinds of love, the love characteristic of Christians is a happy love. This is all the more true because it is infused by the Holy Spirit, who is the source of divine joy (1 Thess. 1:6; Rom. 14:17). And yet, St. Paul reserves for paradise the full flowering of the happiness of loving God and one's brothers. The joy of charity is properly beatitude: to see and to possess completely Him who loves us (1 Cor. 14:12). The joy of this encounter cannot be described (1 Cor. 2:9).

> If then, you have risen with Christ, seek the things that are above, where Christ is seated at the right hand of God. Set your mind on the things that are above, not on the things that are on earth. For you have died and your life is hidden with Christ in God. When Christ, your life, appears, then you shall appear with him in glory (Col. 3:1–4).

Notes

ST. BEDE COLLEGE
LIBRARY
PERU, ILL.

1. Suffice it to recall that the last words of the Emperor Augustus to his wife after fifty-two years of marriage were words of gratitude: "Farewell, Livia, and remember our union."

2. Cf. A. J. Festugière, *L'Idéal religieux des Grecs et l'Evangile* (Paris, 1932), pp. 163–164, from which several of the preceding texts have been borrowed. Cf. also F. C. Grant, *Hellenistic Religions* (New York, 1953) and E. Stauffer, *Le Christ et les Césars* (Colmar-Paris, 1956), p. 229: "It was because Christianity bore witness to the truth in the midst of a deceitful world that it prevailed over the old pagan religions."

3. "The most insignificant and least notable novelists are so imbued with their own importance that they are constantly signing manifestos and deciding questions that could not be further removed from their art." J. Rimbaud, "Pseudochronique d'éducation," *Etudes* (Oct. 1956), p. 105.

4. Rom. 1:18–32. Cf. the commentary of A. Feuillet, "La connaissance naturelle de Dieu par les hommes d'après Rom. I, 18–23," *Lumière et Vie* (1954), pp. 207–224; H. Bietenhard, "Natürliche Gotteserkenntnis der Heiden?", *Theologische Zeitschrift* (1956), pp. 275–288; and L. Cerfaux, "Le monde païen vu par Saint Paul," *Recueil L. Cerfaux* (Gembloux, 1954) II, pp. 415–423, which calls attention to St. Paul's sympathy for his contemporaries. (Cf. however, St. Paul's horror at Athenian idolatry—Acts. 17:16.) But the point of the argumentation in Rom. 1 is precisely the denunciation of the intellectuals who were responsible, not the condemnation of the moral and spiritual values of the pagan world. It has not been suffi-

ciently pointed out that this first chapter is already an apologia of *salvation by faith* (Rom. 1:16–17), and not by philosophic and religious speculation (cf. Mat. 11:25) or by aimless discussions. Rom. 1:18 *et sq.* pertains to the "Greeks" and the "wise men" of verses 14 and 16, who will be saved only by *obedience* to the Gospel (v. 17).

5. St. Jerome's exegesis—"These first-born of the Egyptians seem to me to be the theories of the philosophers by which they retained the men they had deceived and, as it were, captured in their nets" (Ep. LXXVIII, 3)—is echoed in the reflections of J. Conilh, "Les aventures de la philosophie de l'esprit," *Esprit* no. 7–8 (1956), pp. 20–39.

6. Cf. 1 Tim. 4:7, 5:11; Tit. 1:11, 13, 2:15; 2 Tim. 2:23, 3:5.

7. 1 Tim. 1:6, 6:5, 21; Tit. 1:14, 3:11; 2 Tim. 2:18, 3:8, 4:1, 4, 15.

8. 1 Tim. 1:7, 6:20; Tit. 1:16; 2 Tim. 4:3.

9. In a sermon given in July, 1270, at the University of Paris, St. Thomas Aquinas denounces professors who "study philosophy and teach things which are not true in the judgment of faith. When one points out to them that their statements are contrary to the truth of faith, they answer that they only related the words of Aristotle, but that, as for themselves, they affirmed nothing. *Such is the false doctor or the false prophet, for to raise a doubt without solving it is the same as to accept responsibility for it.* This is made clear in Ex. 21:33–34: 'If a man digs a well or uncovers a cistern without covering it again, and an ox or an ass falls into it, then the owner of the cistern must pay the price of the beast.' Now, the man

who raises some doubt in matters relative to faith uncovers a cistern. If he does not resolve the doubt, then he leaves the cistern uncovered, even if he himself keeps a healthy and clear mind and does not fall into error. The listener who has not the same clear mind will be entirely deceived. As a consequence, the professor who has raised a doubt is held in restitution; for it is his fault that the other fell into the trap." *S. Thomas Aquinatis et S. Bonaventurae Balneoregiensis Sermones anecdoti*, ed. P. Uccelli (Modène, 1879), p. 71.

10. 1 Tim. 1:6, 6:4; Tit. 1:11, 3:9; 2 Tim. 2:13, 17, 18, 3:6.
11. 1 Tim. 6:5; Tit. 1:13; 2 Tim. 2:26, 3:9, 4:3–4.
12. 1 Tim. 2:4, 4:3; Tit. 1:1; 2 Tim. 2:25, 3:7; Heb. 10:26.
13. 1 Cor. 15:10: "By God's grace I am what I am, and the grace which entered me was not fruitless. On the contrary I have worn myself out in toil more than any of them. No, not I but the grace of God working with me." Cf. 2 Cor. 2:14, 8:1; and Eph. 3:7–9: "Of that message I was made a minister by the gift of God's grace, which was granted to me in virtue of the exercise of his power. Yes, to me, the very least of all the saints, this grace was given to announce among the Gentiles the Good News of the unfathomable riches of Christ, and to enlighten all men as to what is the wonderful plan, that mystery which has been hidden from eternity in God."
14. Cf. 2 Cor. 3:12; Eph. 3:12; Phil. 1:20; Heb. 3:6, 4:16, 10:19, 25.
15. 1 Cor. 14:18; Phil. 4:16; Col. 4:2; 1 Tim. 2:1.
16. Cf. also St. Augustine, *In Ps. 54* (PLXXXVI, 629) and E. Mersch, "Filii in Filio," *Nouvelle Revue Théologique* (1938), pp. 818, *et sq*.

17. *C. Arianos, III*, 34 (PG XXVI, 396). [The Fathers did not use this terminology with all the precision or the theological implications that these terms received in later theology. The realism of the Fathers could be exaggerated if we lose the historical perspectives of these writings. —Editor's note.]

18. Rom. 8:29. St. Thomas Aquinas comments: "The adoption of the children of God is nothing other than this conformity. Indeed, he who is adopted by God as His child is made conformable to the only Son of God, by participating in His glory" (*Ad Rom. VIII, lect.* 6). "We cannot become the adopted sons of God, if we are not made like to the first-born Son" (*Ad Gal. VI, lect.* 2).

19. St. Thomas Aquinas writes: "The principal element in the Law of the New Testament, that in which all its value lies, is the grace of the Holy Spirit" (I^{a}II^{ae}, q. 106, a.1).

20. PG XXV, 473.

21. Rom. 15:30; 1 Cor. 14:1; 2 Cor. 6:6; Gal. 5:13; Phil. 2:1.

22. 1 Thess. 1:3, 3:6, 5:8; Eph. 6:23; Philem. 5; 1 Tim. 4:12, 6:11.

23. 2 Thess. 3:6, 1 Cor. 4:17, 9:5–6, 11:2, 16; cf. *Recueil L. Cerfaux* (Gembloux, 1954), pp. 253–263.

24. Rom. 1:18–2:16; cf. C. H. Dodd, *New Testament Studies* (Manchester, 1953), pp. 129–142.

25. Rom. 8:2, 11:1 Cor. 15:45; 2 Cor. 3:6; cf. J. Müller, *Der Lebensbegriff des hl. Paulus* (Münster, 1940), pp. 87–96.

26. 2 Cor. 3:18, 4:16; Col. 3:10. Speaking with an old Egyptian priest who put his glory in the immemorial antiquity of his Ancestors, Solon said: "In Greece we remain al-

ways young; in Greece there are no old men!" But the
ideal Solon is truly realized in the Church of Christ.

27. 1 Thess. 1:5; 2 Thess. 2:13; Rom. 15:13, 19; 1 Cor. 2:4,
12:7, 11; Eph. 2:16; 2 Tim. 1:7, etc.

28. G. Didier has written an intelligent study concerning this
problem, although a personal slant is in evidence. Cf. G.
Didier, *Désintéressement du chrétien* (Paris, 1955).

29. It is related that the great exegete Wescott, when ac-
costed by a member of the Salvation Army who asked
him, "Are you saved?" answered: "That depends on how
you understand the word *saved*. Do you mean *sôtheis*,
sesômenos, or *sôzomenos*?" St. Paul does, in fact, use the
verb "to save" in these three tenses: the Christian is already saved by baptism; he is in the process of being saved
all during his life; he will be saved after death. Cf. A. M.
Hunter, *Interpreting Paul's Gospel* (London, 1954), p.
94.

30. Cf. J. Dupont, *L'Union avec le Christ suivant Saint
Paul* (Louvain-Paris, 1952).

31. 1 Cor. 1:7; Phil. 3:20; Tit. 2:13; 2 Tim. 4:8; Heb. 9:28.

32. Gal. 5:22 associates charity and joy inseparably.

33. The verb *agapan* signifies: "to be happy, to rejoice, to
acclaim."

A NOTE ON THE TYPE
IN WHICH THIS BOOK WAS SET

This book has been set in Electra, a type face created in 1935 by W. A. Dwiggins, the well-known Boston artist. This type falls within the "modern" family of type styles, but was drawn to avoid the extreme contrast between "thick and thin" elements that marks most "modern" type faces. The design is not based upon any traditional model, and is not an attempt to revive or to reconstruct any historic type. Since its birth, Electra has met with success because of its easy-to-read quality. This book was composed and printed by the York Composition Company, Inc. of York, Pa., and bound by Moore and Company of Baltimore, Md. The design and typography of this book are by Howard N. King.

THE TRINITY
AND OUR
MORAL LIFE
according to St. Paul
by
Ceslaus Spicq, O.P.

Roman citizenship was important to St. Paul for it brought privileges and powers granted to no other men. Yet with this in mind, after his conversion, Paul tells the community of Philippi, "As for us, our commonwealth is in heaven." Christians thus, he says, are to claim the citizenship of heaven, fully aware of the privileges, powers, and responsibilities of that great destiny.

From the writings of St. Paul, the author shows how the Saint wishes us to live as citizens of heaven in a popular presentation of an astonishingly optimistic Pauline doctrine, which Father Spicq never tires of preaching: "Christians, you are already saved from the moment of your baptism; you are already glorified with Christ here and now." The author first shows how the paganism of the times indicated the necessity of revelation from God and how this revelation came from the Father in the person of Christ in the New Testament. Christians as a result must express their gratitude to the Father by living *in Christ Jesus* a new law of imitation of Christ, a new conception of living which makes of each a new man. This Christian concept of life is not a mere institution or religious economy involving a moral code and an abstract doctrine but it is summed up in the Person from whom it derives its character. How

(continued on back flap)